dining design

informal restaurant design

dining design

informal restaurant design

Showcase Edition

An Imprint of

PBC INTERNATIONAL, INC.

Distributor to the book trade in the United States and Canada:
Rizzoli International Publications Inc.
300 Park Avenue South
New York, NY 10010

Distributor to the art trade in the United States and Canada:
PBC International, Inc.
One School Street
Glen Cove, NY 11542
1-800-527-2826
Within New York State
call 516-676-2727
Fax 516-676-2738

Distributor throughout the rest of the world:
Hearst Books International
1350 Avenue of the Americas
New York, NY 10019

Library of Congress Cataloging-in-Publication Data

Dining design / by the editors of PBC International.--Showcase ed.
p. cm.
Includes indexes.
ISBN 0-86636-275-4
1. Restaurants, lunch rooms, etc.--United States--Decoration.
I. PBC International.
NK2195.R4D56 1993 93-12671
747'.8571'0973--dc20 CIP

CAVEAT—Information in this text is believed accurate, and will pose no problem for the student or casual reader. However, the author was often constrained by information contained in signed release forms, information that could have been in error or not included at all. Any misinformation (or lack of information) is the result of failure in these attestations. The author has done whatever is possible to insure accuracy.

Color separation, printing and binding by
Toppan Printing Co.

Printed in Hong Kong

Typography by
TypeLink, Inc.

10 9 8 7 6 5 4 3 2 1

Contents

Abate Seafood Restaurant

Project Location
Pittsburgh, Pennsylvania

Interior Design
DILEONARDO INTERNATIONAL INC.
Robert J. DiLeonardo, Ph.D./*President*

Photography
WARREN JAGGER PHOTOGRAPHY, INC.

The Abate's fish market is within the straight walled and store-fronted section of this building. The building was deliberately made to look as though it had undergone an expansion period, first being a market, then adding a restaurant, then a bar, etc. Overscale red brick and smooth face gray block were selected as the major building materials to emphasize a straight-forward industrial approach. A set-back of the flat front plane of the building allows for play and breaks the line of a double-tiered awning assemblage accenting the entry and retail section of the structure. The layered awning, blue and green plastic fabric (a color selection mimicking the ocean), is rear-lit to add excitement at night. Above the awning work is a gray block panel, a billboard area upon which large box letters and neon are combined for restaurant and market signage. Neon fish adorn the large store-front windows in the take-out and fish market area of Abate's Seafood. Gloss enamel-painted picnic tables and flags that are pin-mounted to the building are other elements used to activate the setting. The picnic tables and neon move into the interior, and combine with a long list of no-nonsense materials like cement

The main focal point of the restaurant is the large mural painted on canvas and lashed onto pipe.

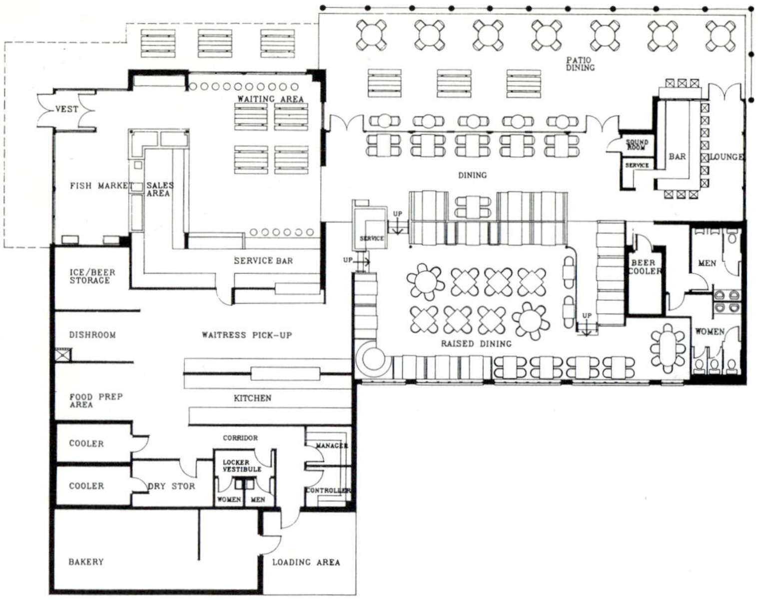

floors, basic white tile and factory shade lights with wire guards.

On the exterior, the sit-down restaurant side of the building is articulated by the use of a low-pitched corrugated metal roof. Large paned, wood mullioned windows and French doors form the perimeter along the front of the building. Windows were deliberately placed high on the rear, allowing for light transmission without having the patrons experience deliveries and kitchen activities. Clerestory windows along the ridge line divides the roof profile and creates interesting interior conditions for the restaurant.

Color and warmth of materials differentiates the dining room and bar, while a simple, almost "rough-hewn" attitude relates back to the take-out market. Many shades of blue and blue-green in gloss and matte finishes were

Scurci
Fresh Daily

Large-paned, wood mullioned windows and French doors form the perimeter along the front of the building.

used on walls, pipe railings, windows and doors, wall panels and trim. Whimsical "party" booths with bowed crowns, and large post ends function as clothes trees. Hardware as well as the enamel paints were selected from marine supply catalogs. Canvas deck chairs and mahogany stained vertical boards, used on booth ends, are other nautical references.

Artwork was kept simple and clear. One important piece, a mural painted on natural canvas that is lashed, hung and weighted with pipe, stretches the entire length of the restaurant. The Escher-esque mural is an adaptation from the artist's study of bird and fish metamorphosis. Museum-cased ship models punctuate booth seating on the raised platform. Marine navigation charts framed in copper, and fish in two and three dimensions were distributed to important focal areas.

Simplicity and clear planning were the ideas that shaped the design for Abate's Seafood.

The takeout and fish market section contains graphic neon signage and vibrantly-painted picnic tables.

Alchemy Ovenworks

Project Location
Providence, Rhode Island

Interior Design
MORRIS NATHANSON DESIGN
Morris Nathanson/*President*
Peter Niemitz/*Vice President*
Blase Gallo/*Vice President–Director of Design*

Photography
WARREN JAGGER PHOTOGRAPHY, INC.

When a young New York couple moved to Providence, Rhode Island, they wanted to start a new business—a bagel bakery that would offer the freshest products. With the assistance of Morris Nathanson, Peter Niemitz and Blase Gallo of Morris Nathanson Design, Pawtuckett, Rhode Island, the couple created an upbeat contemporary bagelry in 1500 square feet. The location is part of a strip shopping center.

Although the space is narrow, the actual square footage is greater than the couple originally anticipated. The additional space is used to seat 60, in addition to cater to a large take-out clientele. The couple also expanded their menu as the business "grew."

Materials throughout are functional and low maintenance. Laminate or tile are used on all the exposed surfaces, allowing for simple clean-up. Take out counters are laminate with chrome edges and ceramic tile fronts. Food display is a dominant element of the interior. The back display wall of products is simple cabinetry painted black. Baskets resting on the counters are filled with fresh baked goods. Glass bottles of beverages stand on the counter. Cakes, pastries and other freshly baked items are behind clear glass.

The baking area is intentionally exposed through windows with dark wood frames. The floor throughout the eatery is black and white mosaic tile with pink tiles dropped in as accents. The patterned white tile continues as a feature above the beaded wood wainscotting. All walls above the wainscotting are finished in gray, black and white zolotone.

A simple gray suspended ceiling accommodates low-voltage track lighting. Halogen wall sconces line the perimeter wall, while large white industrial shades illuminate the food counter.

Food is showcased on and around the Alchemy Overworks counter, brightened with track lighting and lamps under large white shades.

DAILY FAIR
NOVA LOX PLATE
OUR DAILY BREAD
DAILY & NIGHTLY SPECIALS AVAILABLE!!
GARBO
BOGIE
BACALL
KONG
FAY WRAY
ASTAIRE
ROGERS
ABBOTT
COSTELLO
MUFFINS
SOUP
BREW
BAGELS
HENNIEZ

The Arizona Bar & Grill

Project Location
Charleston, South Carolina

Interior Design
CHRIS SCHMITT & ASSOCIATES, INC.
R. Christian Schmitt, AIA, ASID/*Senior Principal*
Christopher A. Rose, AIA/*Senior Associate*
Reginald L. Gibson/*Associate*
Celia Rochford/*Snake Artist*
Lisa Boykin/*Assistant Snake Artist*

Photography
RION C. RIZZO/CREATIVE SOURCES PHOTOGRAPHY

The style, verve, and artistry of the Southwest has invaded Charleston, South Carolina! When Jed Drew's original restaurant of the same name was damaged by fire and Hurricane Hugo, he decided to relocate to a historic railroad warehouse dating from 1864. He challenged local architects Chris Schmitt & Associates, Inc. to combine the already established Southwestern theme of the restaurant with the historic Civil War atmosphere of the warehouse structure to create a new and updated Arizona Bar & Grill.

The designer started by removing the warehouse ceiling to reveal a wonderful timber roof truss system, which was pressure-cleaned with water and left exposed. The brick piers supporting the roof were repaired and also left exposed. The wooden panels between the piers had rotted, so they were replaced with natural redwood to match the original design. The existing floors of heart pine were simply patched, sanded, and sealed.

Since the site had once been a railroad roundhouse, the designer recreated a semicircular courtyard which is continued on the inside of the building by a new, curved red adobe wall. The wall separates the 2,000-square-foot service space from the 4,000-square-foot dining area, which seats 140. The wall is faced with banquettes and incorporates niches for the effective display of the owner's collection of Southwestern art.

To preserve the spatial quality of the warehouse, the functional elements of the restaurant are treated as "objects in the space." They also serve to distinguish the dining, lounge, and bar areas. For instance, the restroom cubicles situated in approximately the center of the restaurant define the diagonal entryway between the lounge and the dining area. These cubicles made of knotty pine panels stained to match the custom-designed tables are joined with galvanized metal brackets and bolts.

The focal point of the restaurant is the magnificent mosaic tile, diamondback rattlesnake, which uncoils across the counter in front of the exhibition kitchen. Snake artist, Celia Rochford, made the head and tail out of pottery over an armature and glazed them to match the glass mosaic tile of the bar top as closely as possible.

The Arizona Bar & Grill has been awarded both the Gold Award and the Grand Award from the Carolinas Chapter of the Institute of Business Designers. Its design emulates the spirit of the Southwest and is certainly an enticing reason for dining with a snake!

The entrance to the restaurant is defined on both sides by the knotty pine panels of the restrooms.

Southwestern art adds to the
ambience of the space.

The zigzag bar made of corrugated galvanized metal and topped with old heart pine is a focal point of the bar/lounge area.

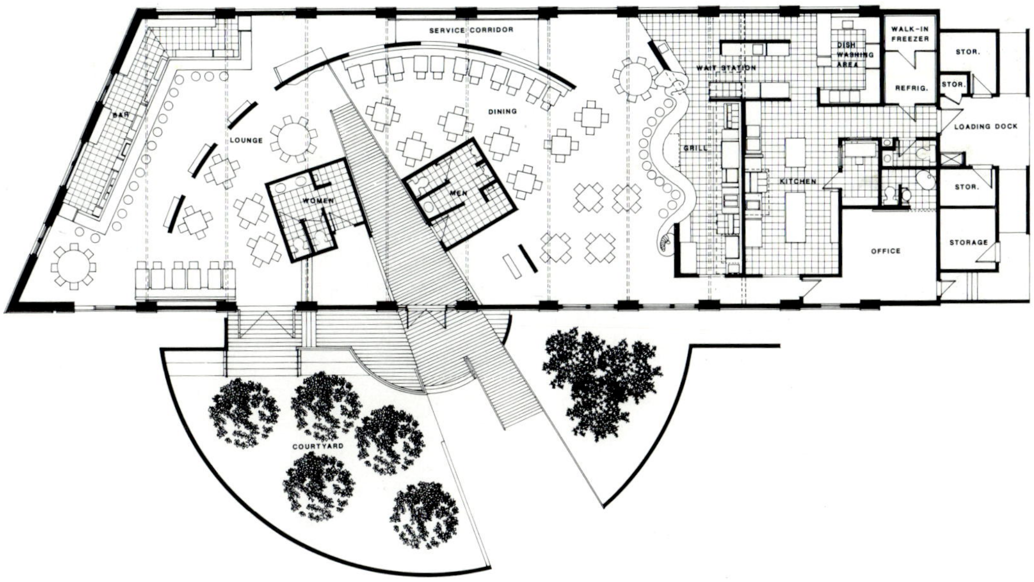

The custom-designed tables are stenciled on top in gold with Indian cave paintings.

The diamond-back rattlesnake counter is faced with corrugated galvanized metal to match the grill hood.

Attitudes

Project Location
Mineola, New York

Client
Mitchell Feurstein

Interior Design
T.M. DESIGN & PLANNING
Mandi QuKay/*designer*

Contractor
BEST FOR LESS

Photography
Carol Bates

When workers at the Pavilion Office Complex in Mineola, New York decide to go out for lunch, they needn't go far. Attitudes restaurant and nightclub, located in the greenhouse structure of the building, offers an upbeat, cosmopolitan atmosphere ideally suited to lunch.

Mandi QuKay of T.M. Design & Planning was instrumental in bringing this ambience to life. The client, Mitchell Feurstein, wanted a space that could cater to the office crowd at lunch time yet be lively and engaging enough to attract nightclub goers in the evening.

The plan of the 204-seat restaurant was affected by the fact that a dropped soffit reduces the ceiling height in the center of the main dining area to an uncomfortably low 7′-6″. The solution was to place the main bar under the soffit forcibly directing traffic around the area. A second bar is located next to the dance floor at the far end of the room. Banquettes and free-standing tables are positioned around the two bar areas.

Seating for the 6000-square-foot restaurant spills from the building into a lushly foliaged, two-story atrium. The focal point of this space is the 50-foot, "natural" rock formation waterfall situated on one wall among the plants. Overhead, hundreds of Tiffoli lights twinkle from the window mullions. The intrinsic beauty of the atrium is underscored by a neutral backdrop of muted lavendar and mauve table tops and a textured, ceramic tile floor. The rich, teal blue color of the chair upholstery provides the only accent.

The well-executed use of neon quickens the atmosphere of the main dining and bar area. Teal blue, semicircular banquettes are emphasized by similarly shaped ceiling soffits outlined in "waves" of vivid lavendar neon. The soffits fade into teal blue fins that rise from the booths' mauve colored end caps. A mirror above each booth sparkles with the reflection of the teal blue neon that outlines the remaining perimeter of the room. The carpet's circular pattern emulates the shape of the booths, and its deep hues of lavendar, mauve and teal counterbalance the brilliant neon lighting.

Attitudes' success as both a luncheon restaurant and a nightclub stands as testimony to its versatile design. Without a doubt, noon or night, it is the place to be in Mineola.

Neon lit soffits over the banquettes impart a sense of intimacy to the main dining area.

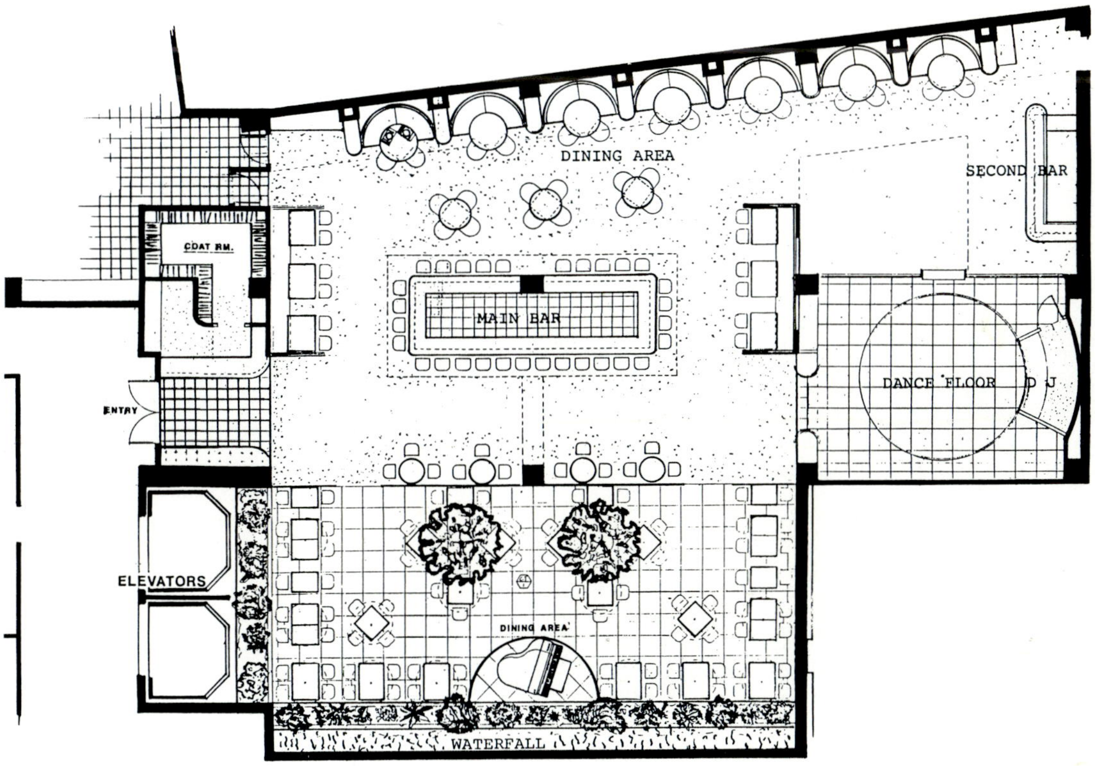

The beautiful atrium may be glimpsed by guests arriving at the restaurant via glass enclosed elevators.

Bee Zee Pizza

Project Location
Danbury, Connecticut

Interior Design
GEORG ANDERSON ASSOCIATES
Georg Anderson/*Principal, ASID, IBD*
Phyllis A. Miley/*Project Designer*

Photography
Don Riley

An outdoor European cafe comes inside in Danbury, Connecticut. In fact, a look inside Bee Zee Pizza is almost like looking outside. By using architectural elements generally associated with exteriors, designers Phyllis A. Miley and Georg Anderson created a 1600-square-foot eatery that's a breath of fresh air.

Creative use of mirrors and decorative blue window shutters create faux windows. Following through with every detail, the designers even added painted white window frames. A skylight lighting system creates an atrium-like setting. A strip of wallcovering, bordered by teal wood molding, brings a colorful pattern to the soffits. Wall fixtures are reminiscent of nighttime illumination at a sidewalk cafe. Set on white stucco walls, the sconces create gentle shadows.

One goal of Anderson and Miley was to create an inviting atmosphere—one that offered instant recognition and eye appeal. Who wouldn't want to step inside? From the neon sign in front to its vibrant, yet soft, colors, the decor is welcoming. Laminate in shades of lavendar and teal complement tile used throughout the fast-food restaurant. The use of laminate also gives the restaurant a European edge. Opting for interesting architectural details, the designers used the 2200-square-foot restaurant, including the kitchen, to create an open, airy plan.

The design team didn't let the space's narrow configuration or the need for an exposed kitchen and serving area hinder them from creating a lively, contemporary place for pizza and other Italian specialities. The serving area includes practical necessities such as a partial marble countertop, pizza ovens and shielded serving trays.

Anderson and Miley turned some possible problems into rewarding solutions. Another goal was to create a durable, easily maintained interior on a restricted budget. The tile floor, in shades of blue, teal, tan and white, is arranged in an alternating diagonal pattern. It's easily cleaned, as are the laminate counters and tabletops.

Mirrors with painted white frames become windows, while giving the illusion of more space.

A view from the outside inside the airy Bee Zee Pizza.

Across from the serving line are tables for two.

Lavendar and teal laminate stripes liven up the serving area, complete with pizza ovens and protected serving trays.

A skylight lighting system brightens the main eating area.

Blakes Ltd.

Project Location
Providence, Rhode Island

Interior Design
LUIGI BIANCO DESIGN ASSOCIATES
Luigi Bianco/*CEO and Principal Designer*
Harold Smith/*Designer*
Ann Howe/*Designer*
Robert Hawkinson/*Consulting Engineer*
Leonard A. Garofalo/*Consultant*

Photography
ROBERT PERRON

A turn-of-the-century country club decor shines through Blake's Ltd., a full-service restaurant and banquet facility. The original 1800 square foot on two floors was expanded to 10,000 square feet on three floors under the direction of designers from Luigi Bianco Design Associates.

The lower level of Blake's includes the offices, bakery, wine cellar and cold storage. The Pub and Billiard rooms are also located here. The main level, where guests enter, includes the reception and waiting area, two dining rooms, and a kitchen. The mahogany bar on the main level features a porch lounge and detailed carving. On the third level, banquet rooms, a service bar, a service and preparation kitchen and storage occupies the space.

The rich decor of Blake's is set in its dark wood tones. White linens add a crisp touch, while wood carvings add one-of-a-kind elegance. Glass ceiling fixtures, wall sconces and summer-time paintings give way to the yacht club feel.

Seaside paintings and the brick fireplace are "homey" extras.

Bolero's Restaurant

at the Radisson Palm Springs Resort and Conference Center

Project Location
Palm Springs, California

Interior Design
COLE MARTINEZ CURTIS AND ASSOCIATES
Jill Cole/*Principal*
Michael King/*Project Director*
Rikki Dallow/*Project Designer*
Mark Sherman/*Designer*

Photography
JAIME ARDILES-ARCE

For 28 years, the Radisson Palm Springs Resort and Conference Center, formerly the Palm Springs Riviera Hotel, has been hostess to most of the major social events worth attending in the vicinity. With 461 rooms, it is the city's largest resort hotel. Recognizing the importance of the property to its location, the owner recently embarked on a $15 million renovation program to restore and enhance the resort's reputation.

The renovation program was accomplished in two phases. The second, and much more comprehensive, phase entailed the complete reconstruction of the resort's public spaces including the restaurant and bar. Cole Martinez Curtis and Associates, the Marina del Rey, California-based interior design firm, accepted the job of reincarnating the 1950's style Radisson into a contemporary resort with a definitely California feel and a timeless look. The challenge was to create this metamorphosis within a moderate budget.

Traffic flow was the first obstacle that had to be overcome. The original entrance to the hotel was on the lower level of the two-story main building, without cues to direct guests into other public spaces. Working in harmony with the architect, the designer took what had been a dimly lit, awkward seating area on the lower level and transformed it into the inviting registration lobby. The upper level, where the circular registration desk once stood, is now a delightful new lobby lounge. To entice guests through the lobby lounge, a tiered fountain and skylights were incorporated into its design. Three skylights at the back of the room illuminate the massive staircase leading down to the restaurant and bar.

The addition of skylights over the staircase allows natural daylight into the interior spaces of the restaurant.

Additional windows and doors provide panoramic views of the mountains during the day and of the play of lights on the pool at night.

Once at the bottom of the stairs, a new flagstone corridor beckons guests to the 132-seat Bolero's Restaurant. The restaurant is light and airy made so by a change in the back elevation of the main building. This change allowed the addition of more windows and doors, which provide the restaurant with exhilarating views of the mountains surrounding Palm Springs and the main pool. To take further advantage of this panorama, a new, 50-seat poolside eating area was created off the dining room. Lightly scaled wicker and rattan furniture and a desert color palette enhance the restaurant's casual, resort atmosphere.

The cocktail lounge is an area where people can wait to be seated in the dining room or just sit with a drink and enjoy the view. For continuity, the bar and restaurant share many of the same design details including natural wood finishes and rattan furniture. A monochromatic color scheme of earthy desert hues is augmented in both spaces by the desert's jewel tones. Splashes of turquoise and purple found in the restaurant are complemented by light lavender and deep shades of rose and terra cotta in the bar.

The transformation of Bolero's Restaurant and, indeed, the entire resort, has been highly successful. The hostess of Palm Springs is back in all her splendor!

The relaxed atmosphere of the bar is the perfect spot for enjoying a drink or waiting to be seated in the restaurant.

Carmine's

Project Location
New York, New York

Interior Design
MORRIS NATHANSON DESIGN, INC.
Morris Nathanson/*President*
Peter Niemitz/*Vice President*
Blase Gallo/*Vice President–Director of Design*
David Jackson/*Designer*

Photography
PETER PAIGE ASSOCIATES INC.

The only way for the Morris Nathanson Design team to create a quintessential neighborhood Italian restaurant in 6600 square feet on a budget of $200,000 was to incorporate as many existing elements into the interior as possible. The space was formerly a 1960's-style Chinese restaurant with lots of red and black vinyl, a hung ceiling, walnut paneling and carpeting. It wasn't until these things were ripped out and thrown away that the designers could find existing materials to work with.

Upon removing the former Chinese restaurant's carpeting, the designers found a hardwood floor that they repaired and stained. The hung ceiling was punched through to reveal architectural details, including grand columns with decorative crowns, coffered ceilings, and soffits and moldings with detailed trims. In keeping with the restaurant's earthy Italian tone and

Existing columns with decorative crowns, coffered ceilings and detailed molding let the designers create an earthy Italian tone on a restricted budget.

Tables are practically touching in the 246-seat Carmine's, which was designed to be the ultimate reflection of neighborhood closeness.

A classic dark wood bar, normally crowded, welcomes Carmine's patrons.

within budget, cracks and some broken pieces were kept in place. The whole room is pulled together by painted walls in warm Tuscan yellow.

Carmine's is located in a densely populated area on Manhattan's upper West side. The area has a distinct neighborhood closeness that the designers wanted to capture in its interior. The outside of Carmine's is simple. In fact, it blends right in.

Existing terrazzo tiles in a checkerboard pattern in the entry were cleaned and restored. Once inside, patrons walk past a busy bar. The classic design includes a dark stained black bar displaying various brands of liquor and glassware on top of the counter. Chrome swivel stools with vinyl padded seats provide comfortable seating at the bar and along the side wall rail.

A half flight of stairs leads from the bar to the large dining room. Tables are placed close together, practically touching each other.

Lighting fixtures in the bar and dining spaces are antiques. They lack conformity which establishes a sense of spontaneity and fun. They also add interest. Numerous portraits and photographs of various Italian activities and celebrations are hung throughout.

Large portions of delicious Italian cuisine served family style in a comfortable, friendly neighborhood setting make the 246-seat Carmine's a popular place in New York City.

A checkerboard pattern of terrazzo tiles leads up to the dining room.

The City Bakery

Project Location
New York, New York

Owner
Maury Rubin

Interior Design
TURETT FREYER COLLABORATIVE ARCHITECTS
Wayne Turett/*Partner-in-Charge*
Catherine Leriche, Bruce Garmendia/*Project Managers*
Anna Cinquemani, Christopher Daly,
Gerardo Fitz-Gibbon, Patrick Williams/*Project Team*

Lighting Consultant
GARY GORDON ARCHITECTURAL LIGHTING

Contractor
GRYPHON CONSTRUCTION

Photography
PAUL WARCHOL

The City Bakery is intended to be a collection of conventional elements packaged in an unexpected, modern way.

The solution attempts to shed the excess conventions of the predictable and the expected. By using mundane and fundamental elements (i.e., metal stud magazine holders) the architects tried to create a new aesthetic. The use of industrial components (stainless steel tables, bulk paper dispenser, menu board, and exposed concrete floors) assembled in a harmoniously new way help to break down the expectations of the traditional bakery. Additionally, the contrast between the 1920s exterior and the clean modern interior heighten the perception of a new order inside. The design and placement of playful, yet, serious elements throughout, serve to create an inviting atmosphere. These elements include five fixed tables with revolving chairs on wheels, coat hooks and menu holders that are simple bolts, fun house mirror, stainless steel pastry display holders, and a wall of cake boxes. The activity of the kitchen gently perceived through the soaring translucent fiberglass walls creates the connection between eating and baking.

The City Bakery is designed within a tall narrow existing 1800-square-foot ground floor space in a circa 1920 mercantile building. Its previous use was as a cut rate carpet store. The Bakery required seating for 38 and the capacity to serve 120 people per hour in take-out trade. The shop was required to directly relate to the unique pastry designs of the owner, Maury Rubin. Mr. Rubin's pastries use traditional Parisian ingredients packaged in a fundamentally modern way. All baking is done on the premises, therefore making the kitchen a dominant design element.

Actual cakeboxes were tied with thin gauge wire and then adhered to the wall, creating an abstract yet fun geometric pattern.

A view of the Bakery through the plate glass window.

kitchen

The kitchen is located behind a transluscent fiberglass wall at the far end of the bakery.

The predominant color of the Bakery is white, with beige and gray accents in the vinyl upholstery.

Cakes and pastry on display add color to the monochromatic interior.

Television studio spotlights were ceiling mounted, thus enhancing the industrial "feel" of this project.

TODAY'S SPECIALS
SOUP
CARROT
SPECIAL PIZZA
HOUSE PIZZA
HOUSE SOUP
TASTY TOMATO

E.J.'s

Project Location
New York, New York

Interior Design
MORRIS NATHANSON DESIGN, INC.
Morris Nathanson/*President*
Peter Niemitz/*Vice President*
Blase Gallo/*Vice President-Director of Design*
David Jackson/*Designer*

Photography
PETER PAIGE

When experienced restaurateurs Eric Levine and Jay Silver obtained adjoining storefronts on Manhattan's Upper West Side, they planned to convert the site into a restaurant. Both spaces, one a former Sushi bar, the other a retail store, together totaled only 1300 square feet. Neither had any architectural merit. Nevertheless, the two partners were undeterred.

Faced with the realities of a small space, a low budget, and a need to maximize seating capacity, the two men turned to Morris Nathanson Design, Inc. for advice. The design team recognized that the location required a restaurant which would appeal to a West Side clientele in search of good, inexpensive food in a relaxed atmosphere.

The recommended solution, a simple coffee shop or luncheonette, proved ideal. Not only is E.J.'s the only luncheonette in the neighborhood, but its 50s theme capitalizes on the revived popularity of old-fashioned diners. The designer's creative manipulation of colors and materials appropriate to the theme compensates for the lack of architecture in the space. In addition, the resulting menu eliminated the need for a kitchen keeping budget and labor costs at a minimum. Most importantly, this solution allowed for a maximum seating capacity of 61 by incorporating counter stools for singles, two seaters and banquette combinations for doubles, and booth seating for larger parties.

The two ordinary storefronts are now a lively aggregate of 50s-style formica, chrome, stainless steel, and vinyl. The original tin ceiling, the restaurant's only redeeming architectural detail, was replaced with a new one that was painted and aged. Formica counter and table tops are rimmed with chrome. Gleaming, chrome framed mirrors, adorned with flamingos, and 50s photographs appear on the walls above authentic looking formica wall panels that are also outlined in chrome. Vivid blue color splashes across the vinyl banquettes and stool seats. Emerald green and the same striking blue intersect to form a merry checkerboard pattern on the vinyl tile floor.

Overnight, E.J.'s has become a popular spot for breakfast, lunch, dinner or even a late night snack. Its immediate success affirms it is no longer just an ordinary place!

The original tin ceiling fell as it was being refurbished. The new one was painted and aged to look old.

The '50s style counter, just inside the entry, is complete with chrome-rimmed stools, a quilted stainless steel wall, and geometric cutouts accenting the soffit.

Filibuster's Bar

Project Location
Indianapolis, Indiana

Location Design
FORMA
Robert Clark/*Senior Interior Designer*

Photography
JOHN VAUGHAN

When Robert Clark began designing Filibuster's in The Westin Hotel, Indianapolis, he was challenged to create a bar and gathering spot that would "stand alone" from the new hotel, and attract both travelers and locals. His approach was to create a pub-like atmosphere—a grand departure from the spacious and bright hotel that's generously filled with windows and skylights.

Dark woods and rich colors create warmth and intimacy throughout the bar. The designer opted for a deep plum, forest green and violet gray scheme, accented by ebonized wood, polished and antique brass, copper and pewter. A large mahogany bar, reminiscent of a 1930s style, is the focal point of the 80-seat meeting place. It was custom designed with a granite top and charcoal black accents. Interesting carved columns frame an extensive liquor collection at the back of the bar.

Mahogany is also found on chairs, stools and banquettes. These pieces are upholstered in loden green fabric with a whimsical pattern of ducks in flight. Lizard-textured vinyl and chenille plaids accent the upholstery.

Granite inserts provide an elegant touch to the hardwood floor. The tin ceiling is surrounded by stepped soffits and hardwood trim. Marbelized grid paper in cranberry, charcoal and cinnamon shades covers the walls and provides a backdrop for abstract artwork and photographs of local sports action and celebrities. Low-voltage halogen lighting accents the artwork. Polished brass wall sconces and antique brass lamps create an intimate glow at table level. Pleated Roman shades cover the tall windows without obscuring the view to outside.

To attract outside business, Filibusters can be entered from the street. There's also an entrance in the hotel's main lobby. This interior entrance is intentionally subtle to create a sense of discovery and enhance the low-key atmosphere of the gathering place.

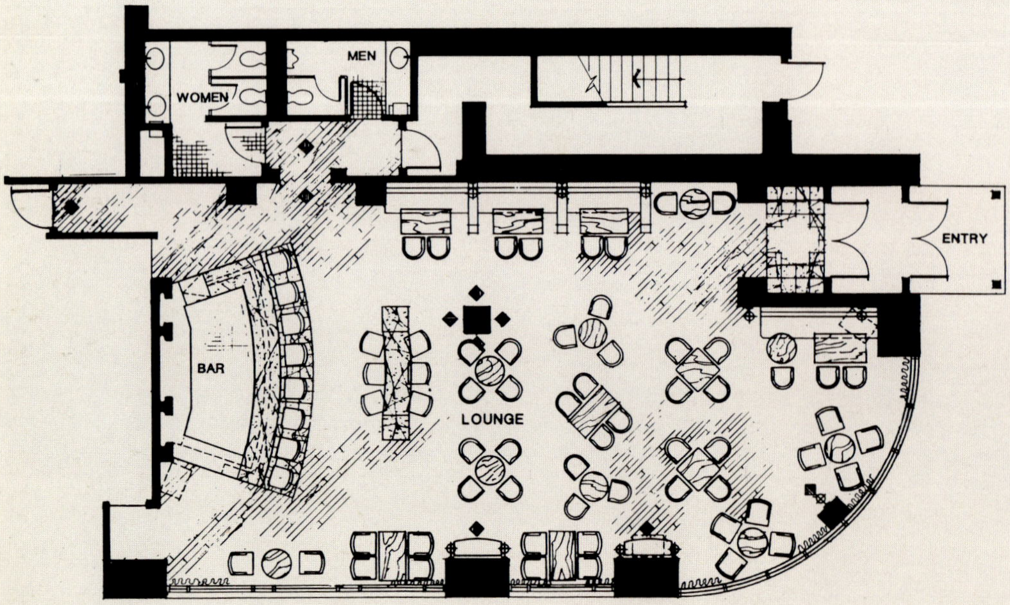

Birds-in-flight upholstery lends a whimsical touch to the 80-seat bar.

Polished brass wall sconces and antique brass lamps provide intimate lighting.

The overall pub atmosphere of Filibuster's is rich, but inviting. It's designed to attract guests of The Westin Hotel in Indianapolis, in addition to locals.

Ground Round/ Lefty O'Rourke

Project Location
New York, New York

Interior Design
TOBIN/PARNES DESIGN ENTERPRISES
Robert Mark Parnes, AIA/*Principal*
Carol Tobin, Associate ASID/*Principal*
Kenn Karseboom/*Project Director*

Photography
JON ELLIOTT

In mid-town Manhattan, Ground Round and Lefty O'Rourke restaurants come together under one roof and share a common kitchen and customer facilities. One thing they certainly don't share, though, is personality. Ground Round is a full-service traditional burger and fries restaurant. It's geared toward family dining. Lefty O'Rourke has a pub-like environment designed primarily with working adults in mind. In fact, the bar/deli was created, from concept to layout, by its owners, The Riese Organization, and designers from Tobin/Parnes Design Enterprises, New York, New York. For interior specialists, Robert Mark Parnes, AIA, Carol Tobin, Associate ASID, and Kenn Karseboom, project director, unifying the two restaurants was a challenge.

The established interior finishes and colors of Ground Round center on neutral earthtones and natural woods. The idea behind Lefty O'Rourke's interior was to create a contemporary and lighter toned version of a typical dark oak Irish pub. Neutral tones with contrasting black wood and natural copper details accomplish this. Colors and materials in both restaurants were carefully selected to harmonize.

A sports theme is the main unifying feature. Sports memorabilia and artifacts are hung as wall decorations throughout the 6383 square foot space. This results in a comfortable atmosphere for both families and professionals who stop in for lunch, dinner or cocktails.

Ground Round from the entrance. Sports memorabilia links the decor of the family restaurant to the more pub-like LeftyO'Rourke.

Houlihan's Old Place

Project Location
New York, New York

Interior Design
TOBIN/PARNES DESIGN ENTERPRISES
Robert Mark Parnes, AIA/*Principal*
Carol Tobin, ASID (Associate)/*Principal*
Kenn Karseboom/*Project Director*

Photography
JON ELLIOTT

When creating a full-service restaurant in a space that had been a late night rock-and-roll club, its interior designers decided to restore "the old" before toying with "the new." To begin with, the striking three-story building has 18′ tall windows that were partly obstructed and blackened. Many other architectural details had also been hidden or partly destroyed.

The design team from Tobin/Parnes Design Enterprises, New York—Robert Marke Parnes, AIA, Carol Tobin, Associate ASID, and Kenn Karseboom, project director—went floor by floor when restoring aged details for a new, fresh interior. On the first floor, the designers cleaned up carved plaster pilasters framing mirror panels which soar to the second floor ceiling through the stair well. The grand stairway, still with its original baluster of brass and stainless steel with glass panels and cylinders, leads to the second level.

An acoustical ceiling was removed from the second floor to reveal the original sloping ceiling to the 18-foot-high windows facing Fifth Avenue. The 7700 square foot restaurant also includes a rooftop banquet space and kitchen facilities in its cellar.

Most of the interior of Houlihan's Old Place is based on company specifications. The designers, however, made slight modifications in keeping with the newly restored architectural details of the interior.

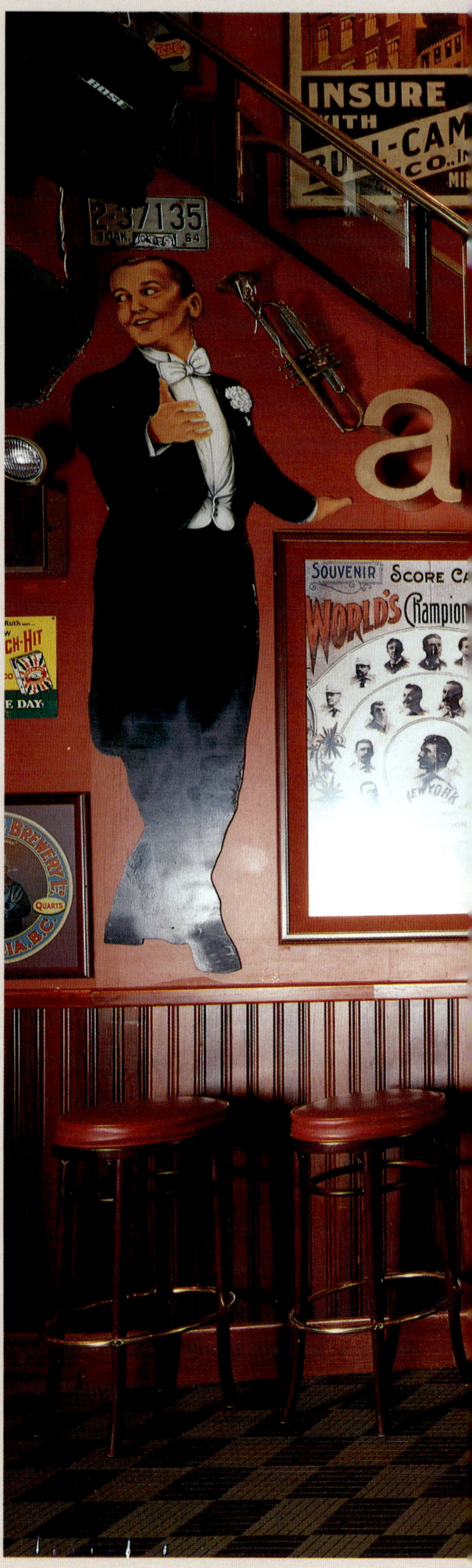

Carved plaster pilasters soar to the ceiling of the second floor. A grand staircase leads to another dining area.

CELUI DES CONNAISSEURS
BASS
CIRCUS
1, 2, 3, 4 and 6,7

Eighteen-foot windows on the
second level face Fifth Avenue.

I Cugini Ristorante

Project Location
Santa Monica, California

Interior Design
HATCH DESIGN GROUP
Jeff Hatch, Sam Hatch, Jackie Hanson

Photography
MILROY/McALEER

Inspired by timeless Italian design, I Cugini Ristorante reflects traditional styling in a fast-paced twentieth century setting. Jeff Hatch, Sam Hatch and Jackie Hanson paid careful attention to blending the past with the present. The goal for the designers from the Hatch Design Group, Santa Monica, was to create an inviting decor that would attract a vast array of clientele, while establishing a separate identity for the restaurant, located in a high-rise building.

The interior features warm, classic elements found in an old Italian family restaurant—quite a departure from its modern limestone exterior. Marble, terrazzo, scrolled iron work and woven tapestries in cream, black and russet evoke a historical quality brought up to date with contemporary finishes, including faux patterns resembling stone, hand-textured walls and granite.

Murals, painted above the wainscotted walls, line the serpentine booths to add drama. The murals were painted by Doug Bowman, of Pasadena, California, who restores historical works of art and architecture. Wainscotting is douglas fir with two coats of stain.

Delicately painted sheaths of wheat and flowers adorn the soffits and barrel vaulted ceiling. To create a less formal elegance, large-scale parquet flooring was used in cherry and hickory. This adds a rustic flavor to the 8975-square-foot space. Low-voltage lighting and custom iron and alabaster chandeliers create a warm glow no matter what time of day or night. Daylight is maximized through an attached patio that offers a magnificent ocean view. The patio resembles a European bistro.

Most important in a great Italian restaurant is the cooking, and it's given special attention in an exhibition-style area. Here an attached bakery and wood-burning pizza oven bring the art of traditional Italian cooking methods to the forefront. The restaurant seats 255.

The bakery for take-out bread, pastries, coffee and expresso.

Salads and desserts are made in the pantry.

An exhibition kitchen, complete with scrolled iron work.

A vaulted ceiling in one of the dining areas is reminiscent of traditional Italian design.

In Prov

Project Location
Providence, Rhode Island

Interior Design
MORRIS NATHANSON DESIGN, INC.
Morris Nathanson/*President*
Peter Niemitz/*Vice President*
Blase Gallo/*Vice President–Director of Design*

Photography
WARREN JAGGER PHOTOGRAPHY INC.

In the heart of the downtown Providence financial district, there's only one place to enjoy a tapas menu while doing some serious people watching. The place to be is In Prov, located on the first floor Galleria of The Fleet Center office and retail complex. In Prov has the flavor of a European cafe, and the look of an intimate, upscale gathering place.

In Prov, set within three walls of glass, is only accessible from inside the Galleria. The entrance resembles a sidewalk cafe with small tables covered by custom umbrellas. Once inside, the design features separate areas that are all within view of the others. The bar is located next to the entrance and in full view of people walking through the Galleria. This leads to spur-of-the-moment walk-in traffic, just what the restaurant's owners and interior designers had in mind. The bar has a sloped light canopy that conceals a storage mezzanine. Another focal point of the restaurant is an open food prep, rotisserie area and dessert display that the bar wraps around.

Diners in the main raised eating area can view just about all of the 1400 square foot space, including the exposed kitchen. The dining platform is near the windows overlooking the street, making people watching easier

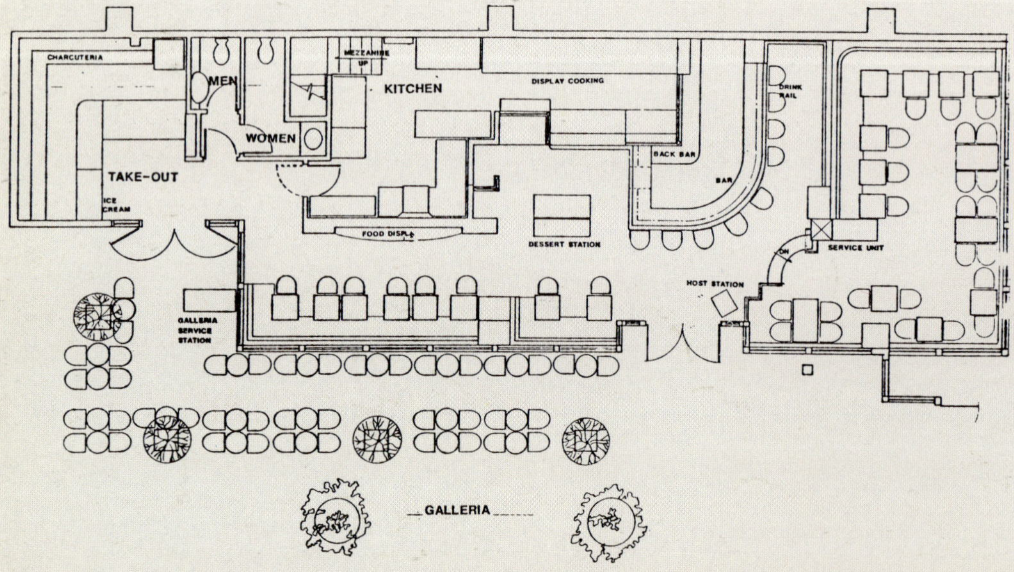

A view from the "sidewalk cafe" into In Prov.

The mahogany bar and faux marble walls are upscale touches.

and even more natural. Open table arrangements make accommodating groups, while not interrupting the view, feasible.

The materials and textures used throughout In Prov result in a sophisiticated decor. Walls are faux marble in beige, white and cream. A stepped plaster ceiling reflects the actual design of the Fleet Center tower. Low-voltage track lighting in a continuous coffer keeps the atmosphere warm and highlights tables and displays. Millwork is black lacquer and rich mahogany. The flooring was selected to match the granite floor of the Galleria—another subtle invitation into the restaurant.

Furnishings include simple black chairs accompanying black laminate tables with stainless steel inlays and mahogany edges. The restaurant seats 110.

The bar wraps around an exposed food preparation, cooking and rotisserie area, viewable from the main dining area.

Low-voltage lighting in a continuous coffer illuminates displays, while showcasing materials.

Le Grande Cafe

Project Location
Boston, Massachusetts

Interior Design
MORRIS NATHANSON DESIGNJ
David Jackson/*Designer*
Morris Nathanson/*President*
Peter Niemitz/*Vice President*
Blase Gallo/*Vice President–Director of Design*

Photography
WARREN JAGGER PHOTOGRAPHY INC.

Nestled in Boston's Back Bay area, with a view down Boylston Street to Trinity Church, is Le Grand Cafe—a European bistro come stateside.

When the restaurant's owners Jack Benjamin and Jerry Green leased the property they knew exactly what they wanted. Besides the location and a cafe decor, they sought to accommodate the local office crowd and neighborhood. They wanted a take-out business, unlike a typical deli, in addition to interior seating. An outdoor seating area was another request.

Today, Le Grand Cafe features fresh foods, bakery goods, breads and rotisserie cooking for take-out or on-site dining. And in warmer months, seating for 20 outside allows patrons to enjoy the weather, while increasing the restaurant's visibility.

The main obstacles facing the restaurant's designers from Morris Nathanson Design, Pawtuckett, Rhode Island, were budget and pre-existing conditions. Le Grand Cafe's layout is long and narrow. A long marble countertop that runs the length of the space had to remain, although it was reworked to fit into the new design. In addition, more seating was needed. An inset was added to the counter, allowing for more stools or individual dining. The counter was shortened which increased equipment space required for the take-out business. A new bakery case, a European style deli case to display gourmet salads, and a rotisserie were added. Counter seating also was added along the length of the restaurant's left wall.

A raised platform area in the back allows for additional tables and lends to the bistro-like atmosphere. Here carpet, Viennese style chairs, and French Impressionist paintings were added.

French lace is used in the front windows. More seating was added in the storefront area, taking advantage of all the available space. Brick walls were painted off-white to retain texture and old-world elegance. A variation of a checkerboard floor pattern is done in blue, gray and white. Tile is also used as decorative accents and wall covering above the counter. The back bar is resurfaced in tile.

To make the interior seem less narrow, oversized mahogany mirrors were added along the left wall. The mirrors were sandblasted, a less expensive alternative to achieve a beveled look. Existing tables were stained. Lighting was retained, and additional fixtures were specified. The iron grillwork was painted for a clean look.

The 1700-square-foot cafe seats 80, plus 20 outdoors. Its interior design blends old world charm with modern freshness for a successful, aesthetically appealing result.

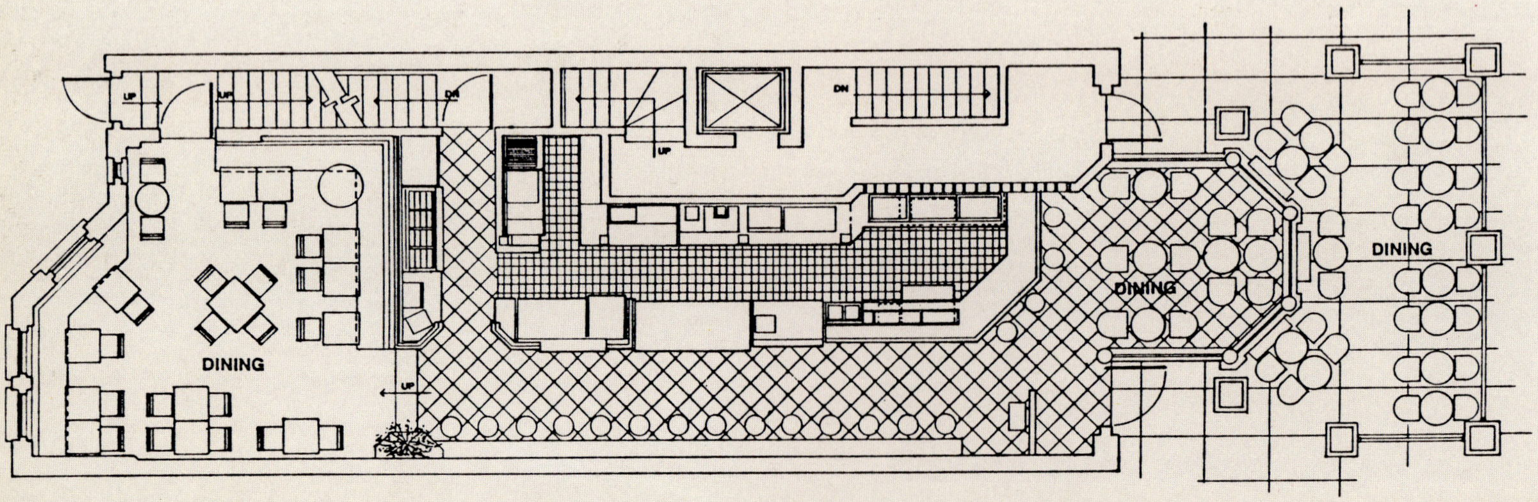

A fixed marble counter runs the length of Le Grand Cafe and provides a place for picking out and picking up fresh bread, salads, pastries and other specialities.

A counter and stools were added to one wall of the cafe to increase interior seating capacity to 80.

Carpeting, Viennese style chairs and paintings combine to make old world charm fresh and new.

L'Opera

Project Location
Long Beach, California

Interior Design
HATCH DESIGN GROUP
Jeff Hatch, Rick McCormack, Melinda Shriver

Photography
Don Romero

In Italian "L'Opera" means masterpiece. In downtown Long Beach, California, L'Opera restaurant—from its decor to its cuisine—has become a masterpiece in itself. Here, contemporary meets traditional.

For designers at Hatch Design Group the challenge was to create an art gallery ambiance in 5200 square feet. Because the space had been occupied by a bank and was located on the ground level of a six-story historical landmark building, the task was somewhat complicated.

The design team opted to keep the space open, rather than breaking it up with visual barriers. Hardwood flooring, high ceilings and white painted walls and ceiling create the effect. Striking green columns are faux marble. New materials complement traditional elements throughout the restaurant. The interesting ceiling pattern was already there, although some was missing. The ceiling was restored by duplicating the molding. Floral upholstery on mahogany chairs and stools add a delicate touch. Mahogany and black granite are used on the bar; the restaurant even includes an exhibition kitchen.

More contemporary materials in the cocktail lounge help separate it from the dining room. Ground and polished concrete stained with iron sulfate is used in place of oak on the floor. Iron sulfite warms the usually cold concrete, while tying it together with the mahogany fixtures. The traditional light fixtures of the dining room are replaced with clusters of individual pendant lights. This creates an illusion of chandeliers.

The building, according to the interior designers, did present unusual obstacles. One challenge was to incorporate a structural brace, which was added to the building during renovation for seismic stability. The solution was to allow the brace's unusual form to become a design element instead of hiding it. The brace was wrapped with drywall for fire protection. Then, the areas between the structure's legs were filled with clear glass with a sandblasted image of Roman columns and pediments. This not only transformed the brace, but also created a gateway between the dining room, bar and kitchen.

Another difficulty was meeting California's handicapped accessibility standards. The restaurant is raised 36" above street level and had no provisions for physically disabled access. The building's exterior couldn't be altered with ramps because of its historical placement, so a mechanical lift was installed off an exit corridor at street level that can raise wheelchairs to the restaurant level.

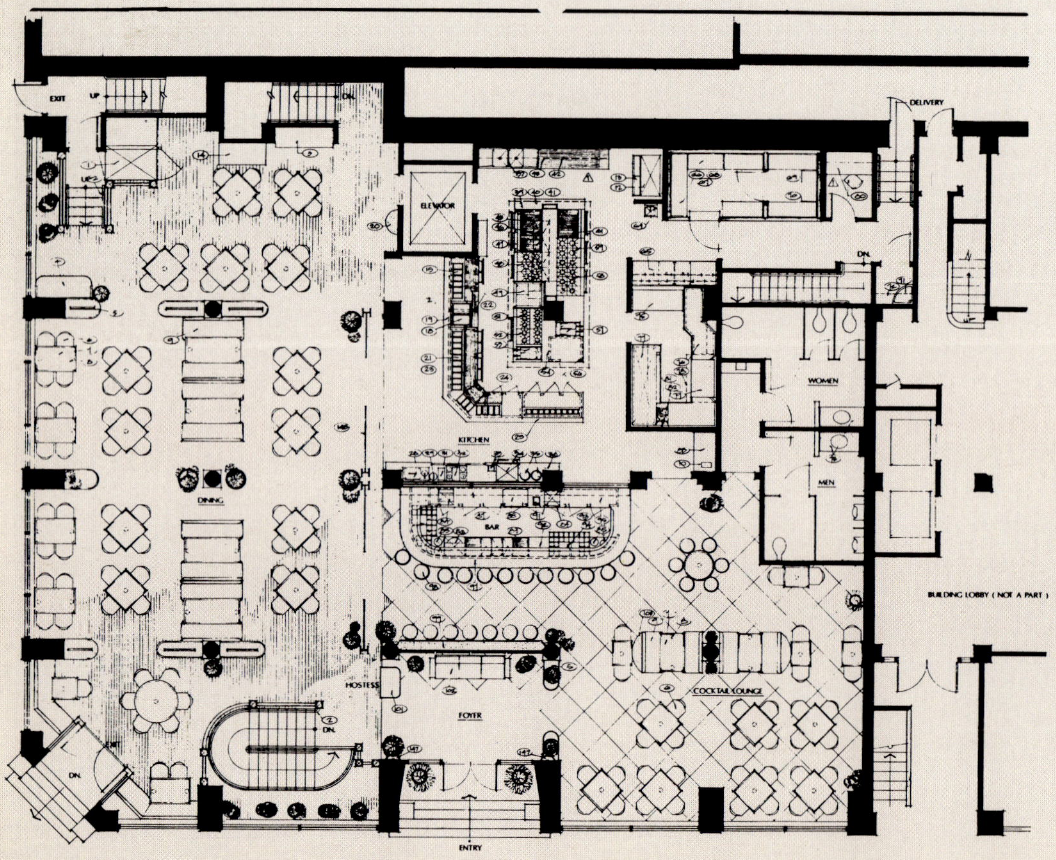

The entrance into L'Opera reflects its historic past.

Individual hanging pendant lights and a concrete floor treated with iron sulfite help separate the bar from the dining area.

A view of L'Opera's main dining room with the exhibition kitchen in the background.

McDonald's at A&S Plaza

Project Location
New York, New York

Interior Design
SILVER & ZISKIND/MOUNT
Charles Morris Mount/*principal*
Jennifer Wellman/*project designer*
POLISHED ALUMINUM CEILING SIMPLEX CORP.

Photography
NORMAN McGRATH

If Steven Spielberg and George Lucas teamed up to design the interior of a McDonald's restaurant, it might look like the one in midtown Manhattan at the A&S Plaza. Charles Morris Mount and Jennifer Wellman used glass, neon and mirrors to create an exciting design in jewel tones. The restaurant is owned by Irwin Kruger, owner of five other McDonald's locations. Three of them were designed by Mount, whose style is to create award-winning "restaurant theater."

Kruger's newest McDonald's is located on the concourse level of the A&S Plaza shopping mall, at the entrance of busy subway and train stations. The space is glass enclosed and lit with bright neon colors and incandescent light reflected in stainless steel acoustical ceiling panels and mirrored walls. In the dining room, the unique and innovative use of neon, placed behind transparent, custom ribbed glass tiles, creates the illusion of a "cosmic" sculpture within the walls.

Columns of silvery amethyst and "diamond" colored reflective tile support the neon studded reflective ceiling. The custom tile floor in a grid pattern with checkerboard border encompasses tones of onyx, turquiose and amethyst. Red neon in the facade of a granite serving counter resembles a glowing hearth. This is accomplished by placing neon between red laminate and brushed stainless steel perforated panels, bordered with polished gun metal steel.

Twelve order stations serve hungry patrons. Here, scrolling menu boards, along with point-of-purchase graphics, were installed. Tables are topped with laminate, and along with booths and banquettes, offer diners a variety of seating options. Stool and banquette covers are aquamarine. Those seated at the counter, made of stainless steel, solid surfacing and illuminated glass tile, overlook a large fountain in the center's atrium. Mirrored walls and an etched glass "wave" panel with an internal neon sculpture are dramatic additions.

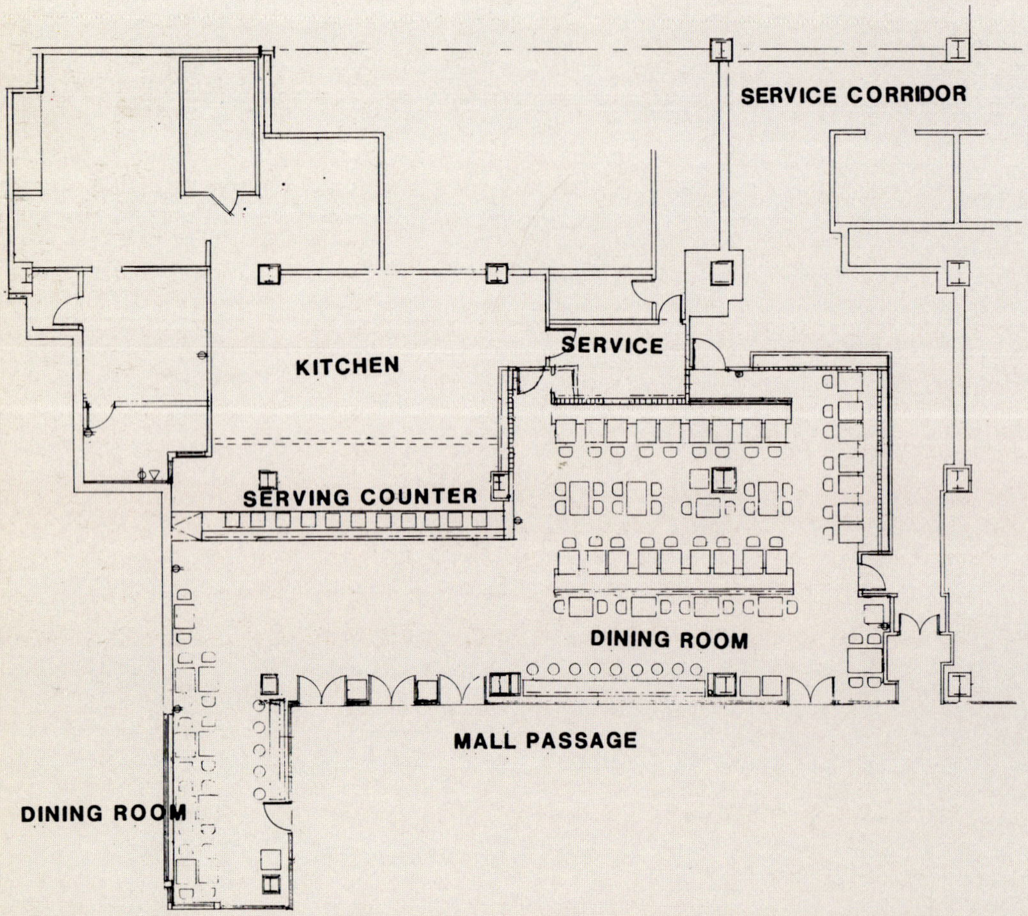

The "Golden Arches" are modernized.

Ample seating, including contemporary white laminate tables contrasted by black chairs, is provided for hungry patrons.

McDonald's at the A&S Plaza in New York City.

Neon, mirrors and jewel tones set the stage, and steal the show.

A ceramic grid pattern on the floor visually adds space to the dramatic design of the fast-food hot spot.

Mr. Steak

Project Location
Winston-Salem, North Carolina

Interior Design
CHARLES MORRIS MOUNT

Photographer
SCOTT FRANCES

Mr. Steak is part of a family-style restaurant chain located in Winston-Salem, NC. The parent company is based in Denver, Colorado. It has a limited menu, featuring steak, hamburgers, and all the trimmings. The decor was rather plain, unpretentious and "truck driver proof." Though sales were well above average for the chain, the client expressed a wish to maintain their present customer base and profile while also broadening their appeal to include businessmen's lunches as well as families, "senior diners" and young couples for dinner.

The renovation was phased over a seven year period as revenues accrued. This time span enabled Mr. Steak to remain open throughout construction.

The original dining room was remodeled and renamed the Burgundy Room. An outdoor dining courtyard and bar was also added to give the building an interesting and appropriate entrance area as well as additional holding and dining space for the increased numbers of customers. Seventy-five seats were gained during this phase. The courtyard runs parallel to a heavily traveled avenue and is protected by vegetation and a decorative wood fence. In the original room, only the stone wall at the end of the room remains. Booths at the windows overlook the courtyard. The floor is carpet and quarry tile. The wood throughout is limed, solid ash. Red Levanto marble reinforces the burgundy theme.

The terrace entry welcomes the patron where the hostess can direct him to either dining area or bar. The walls are ash wainscotting with soft green vinyl wallcovering and quarry tile on the floor.

The bar is located on a raised platform overlooking the entry and the main Greenhouse dining room. The floor is carpeted. The bar is solid ash with a verde green marble top. The ceiling, covered with mirrored simplex steel tiles, incorporates two eight-foot-diameter skylights.

The greenhouse main dining room consists of two dining areas. The upper level is outlined by an enameled steel arbor with suspended lights and plants. The ceiling soars to 27 feet. There are exposed trusses, high-tech track lighting and mirror in a grid pattern to echo the exterior courtyard elements.

The lower dining area is also outlined with the arbor structure and is defined by a beautiful brick wall, accented with brass lighting fixtures and terra cotta planters. Carpet is used here for its warmth and acoustical qualities. Major planting, highlighted by an unusual fig tree, architectural in form, completes the greenhouse setting.

The client has quadrupled gross sales since renovation.

Live plantings in the Greenhouse main dining room continue the atrium/greenhouse theme predominant throughout the entire restaurant.

Exposed trusses draw the eye upward and highlight the soaring 27-foot ceiling.

The bar is located on a raised platform overlooking the entry and the main Greenhouse dining room. Visible in this photograph is one of the two eight-foot-diameter skylights.

Brass wall sconces add a beautiful touch to the brick wall in the lower dining area.

Ollie's

Project Location
New York, New York

Interior Design
MORRIS NATHANSON DESIGN
David Jackson/*Designer*
Morris Nathanson/*President*
Peter Niemitz/*President*
Blase Gallo/*Vice President–Director of Design*

Photography
WARREN JAGGER PHOTOGRAPHY INC.

Ollie's—a Chinese restaurant with an English name and an uptown interior. The 1700 square foot restaurant is located in a busy New York City neighborhood. Anticipating a solid amount of foot traffic at the location, the designers from Morris Nathanson Design decided to relate much of the interior to sidewalk. So even if you're outside the restaurant, you get a feel for what's going on inside.

The storefront windows were entirely reworked. Large sheets of plate glass, framed by glass block pilasters, create an uninterrupted view to passersby and diners alike. An open display kitchen offers maximum food and preparation display. Poultry, vegetables and cooking utensils hung from the open kitchen wall add interest. A kitchen staff working quickly with their hands to create fresh Chinese delicacies is a site to be seen. A menu can be read from the street, which helps lure walk-in business.

Ollie's, located on a busy New York City Street, is brightly lit and wide open to attract walk-in business.

A half-wall covered with earthtone tiles and topped with rippled glass serves as a divider between diners and the kitchen.

A working kitchen and food preparation center is visible to diners and from the street.

The food counter and open kitchen stretch nearly the full length of the restaurant and work as a unifying element. Rippled glass with aluminum frames serve as section dividers and separate diners from the kitchen without interfering with visibility. The designers intentionally stayed away from red laminate and other typical design elements, including hanging lanterns. Warm golden tones are used for all tilework, walls and the oak and pine furniture. Selected pieces of Oriental artwork hung on the walls are the only indications that one is inside a Chinese restaurant. The overall result is a sophisticated, uplifting design that seats 112 people.

Glass windows framed by glass block allow a look inside of Ollie's, a Chinese restaurant with an English name and uptown decor.

Rippled glass and aluminum are section dividers.

The Original A-1 Border Beanery, Bail Bonds & One Hour Perms

Project Location
Chicago, Illinois

Interior Design
MARVE COOPER DESIGN
Marve H. Cooper/*Principal*

Photography
MARK BALLOGG/STEINKAMP & BALLOGG

It's a cross between a junkyard and a Mexican border cafe, and owner Richard Melman likes it this way. Melman and his Lettuce Entertain You organization's tradition of festive theme restaurants continues in The Original A-1 Border Beanery, Bail Bonds and One-Hour Perms. And nothing would suit a restaurant with such a unique name better than a one-of-a-kind interior design.

Melman called upon Marve H. Cooper, Marve Cooper Design, to combine the zany and wonderful. The

Mixed, matched and unmatched artifacts give the Tex-Mex restaurant its relaxed atmosphere.

Exposed beams and pipes in dimmed lighting make for down-home casual dining in the heart of Chicago.

10,000-square-foot space is in an interior mall. Thus, the entrance to the Tex-Mex eatery had to have a strong identity. That it does. Brick, aged wood, old steel drums and a few tires in front of The A-1 Border Beanery set the tone for what awaits inside.

Because of time and budget limitations, Cooper and Melman worked closely together and on the spot. Cooper sketched during discussions. Tradesman and artists worked alongside the designer. All the materials had to be available immediately, and art and artifacts were bought at local junkyards. In the main dining room, walls are peeling and the lights are dimmed. Some tables match, while others don't. Some even have tablecloths. Uneven wood shutters and neon beer signs add to the mismatched interior.

The restaurant includes two bars, two pool tables and video games. If it's interior could talk, it would be screaming, "Kick back, and relax." The restaurant even has an outdoor veranda that has a more subdued decor. All the tables have tablecloths—in one of two shades of pink. There are even flowers on the tables.

Inside the restaurant is a "back porch" complete with a rocking chair and piano. The area doubles as a bandstand.

COLD BEER
CERVEZA FRIA
CORONA
DOS EQUIS
LONE STAR
MILLER LITE
NEGRA MODELO
MESQUITE

The Original A-1 Border Beanery, Bail Bonds and One-Hour Perms.

A view of the entrance to the dining room through the "alley way."

Owen Brennan's Louisiana Grill

Project Location
Memphis, Tennessee

Interior Design
MORRIS NATHANSON DESIGN, INC.
Morris Nathanson/*President*
Peter Niemitz/*Vice President*
Blase Gallo/*Vice President–Director of Design*
David Jackson/*Designer*

Photography
WARREN JAGGER PHOTOGRAPHY INC.

The contemporary exterior of the restaurant was softened with the addition of French doors and the canopy.

America's geography is a changin'. New Orleans has moved to Memphis, Tennessee! Rather, at the very least, Louisiana can lay claim to the 8000 square feet of Memphis that is now known as Owen Brennan's Louisiana Grill.

The inspiration behind this great new Cajun and Creole restaurant is Burt Wolf, the internationally syndicated television food reporter. Wolf's marketing strategy called for the development of a prototype that eventually could be adapted to locations in 23 cities throughout the Southeastern United States. Memphis was selected as the site for the debut of the chain because Wolf felt that many of the locals were already familiar with New Orleans and the name Brennan's.

Wolf commissioned Morris Nathanson Design, Inc. to create the prototype. This task was made even more formidable by the fact that the restaurant was to be located in a new, contemporary office/shopping complex.

To soften the building facade, French paned windows and French doors were installed along two sides. The client persuaded the building owner to create an exterior garden juxtaposing one wall of French doors. In good weather, the garden provides additional seating for 85 and can be viewed by inside diners, as well. During dreary weather, the mirrored panes of the French doors allow the interior to remain bright and cheery.

As they step inside the restaurant, guests are instantly swept up by the excitement of Mardi Gras and the romance of New Orleans. Turning what could have been an architectural problem into an advantage, the designer utilized the 24-foot ceilings to create a "second story" effect. Faux windows with

Custom-designed chandeliers, pendant lights, and oak furniture are reminiscent of the grand scale of a Southern hotel lobby.

louvered shutters look down, while ceiling fans whirl. Multilevel sections, carved out of the large, open dining area, break up the space and bring the ceiling down to more human scale. The wrought iron railings that define the platform areas and appear on the balconies overhead further validate the illusion of the beautiful French Quarter.

The casual materials used throughout the restaurant infuse it with a "saloon" flair. The off-white walls and beaded wood wainscotting provide a neutral background for the dark oak bar, oak furniture, and colorful upholstery and carpeting. Seating is upholstered in bright red, leatherlike vinyl. The plentiful artwork on the walls depicts scenes from New Orleans' Latin Quarter, jazz celebrations, and Mardi Gras festivals, and are all "askew" for a comfortable, take-it-easy feeling.

The piece de resistance of the restaurant, however, are the genuine

The plentiful artwork imbues the restaurant with a saloon flair. Don't miss the haphazard arrangement to further impart a "come as you are" aura.

festival artifacts, which were purchased from original Mardi Gras floats and carnival makers. The spirit of New Orleans comes alive in the unfurled flags, the beautiful crown atop the bar, and the golden cherubs flying over the 200-seat dining area. Authentic carnival bunting, rich with color, drapes from the arms of the carnival man as he peers down from his perch high overhead. At any moment, he will pass by in the parade as the crowd cheers on and the jazz bands play.

The private dining or Audubon Room, named for the Audubon prints found here, can be closed off of the main dining area by French doors.

The harsh appearance of the acoustical ceiling tile was softened by adding ceiling coffers.

Pizzeria Uno

Project Location
Orlando, Florida

Interior Design
MORRIS NATHANSON DESIGN
Morris Nathanson/*President*
Blase Gallo/*Vice President of Design*
Peter Niemitz/*Vice President*
David Jackson/*Designer*

Photography
WARREN JAGGER PHOTOGRAPHY INC.

The prototype of Pizzeria Uno was created by Morris Nathanson Design Inc., Pawtucket, Rhode Island. The firm has also designed several individual franchise locations—each different but similar. When the firm was asked to handle the interior of Pizzeria Uno in Orlando, its owner requested a Southern decor—not country, not Caribbean, but true hospitable and relaxing Southern. To achieve this, Morris Nathanson, Peter Niemitz, Blase Gallo and Designer David Jackson

Neon creates a festive environment during the day and at night. After dark, the colorful lights in the window keep the second-story restaurant in view. The neon can be seen from four blocks away.

Intimate booth seating, mint green and a lot of tile lend a comforting Southern feeling to the interior.

focused first on colors and materials, and then on lighting.

Walls are painted white, and the beaded wood detail is painted mint green. Tiles, popular and plentiful in the South, are used throughout the pizzeria's interior. Black, gray and white tiles create a square pattern on the floor, and glossy black and white tiles adorn the walls. Bright colors are used as accents on the bar, and a taste of the tropics is seen in the colors of neon lighting used extensively inside the restaurant.

Pizzeria Uno is located on the second floor of a building in Orlando's Church Street Station. Local building requirements restrict exterior signage. To compensate for the lack of outdoor "name dropping," the designers kept two glass walls open to the outside and used enough neon inside to be seen for four blocks in the evening. Neon makes the interior fun for diners. It also helps keep Pizzeria Uno part of the Church Street Station, popular during the day and a hot spot at night, scene, literally.

Because two glass walls are open to the outside, venetian blinds were specified. This allows for outdoor viewing in the evening and those daytime hours when the sun isn't at its strongest. It's through the glass walls that neon shines from the inside out.

The bar in Pizzeria Uno is placed near the entrance. Its large octagonal shape creates ample space for stools and a comfortable lounge area. The lounge, located to the right of the bar, is used to handle an excess bar crowd at night, afternoon diners or patrons awaiting an available table. Dining areas surround the bar and lounge. A rear

dining room offers booth seating and a lowered ceiling. The result is a more intimate dining experience.

Booths are used extensively throughout the interior.

To compensate for the hard surfaces used throughout Pizzeria Uno and a relaxed (and sometimes loud) clientele, acoustical tile is used on the ceiling. Pizzeria Uno in Orlando is 5500 square feet. It seats 225.

Dining space surround the large octogonal bar.

Customized railings incorporating the Uno name set one dining area apart from the bar.

Plaza Proenza

at Lindo Mexico

Project Location
Chicago, Illinois

Interior Design
MARVE COOPER DESIGN
Marve Cooper/*Owner*

Photography
Mark Ballogg/Steinkamp & Ballogg

Lindo Mexico is one of Chicago's oldest and most respected full service Mexican restaurants. It began as a simple storefront, 35 seat neighborhood restaurant in 1977 to what is now 416 seats encompassing three connecting downtown buildings.

When the owner decided it was time for the next expansion he told the designer that the new design should set a style that would be used to rehab the three original dining rooms and bar since they were worn and lacked continuity.

After observing the operation, the designer felt the classic cuisine and style of service was reminiscent of fine dining restaurants in Mexico. Also, because the configured space of the addition, the new building would be freestanding (connected to one of the original buildings through a passageway from the bar.), and since an outdoor patio was required and its most likely location would be between the addition and another of the original buildings, the plan was a natural for a *hacienda* and civic plaza.

Designs for a 17th Century from the Colonial period building complete with *corredor* and plaza were presented and

The entrance to the restaurant is marked by wrought iron gates, a black wrought iron bench and plants in vivid Mexican pottery planters—reminiscent of a hacienda terrace.

accepted. To be successful the design had to capture the romance and gentle charm that is so typically Mexican.

Natural lighting was to be relied on as much as possible with well positioned incandescent and candlelight to make up for the harsh light of Chicago winters and to bring out the warm tropical Mexican colors. Close attention to architectural detail was necessary if the restaurant guests were to be transformed into another time and place. To accomplish this, stone fountains and columns were commissioned in Mexico by the designer. Handcrafts such as rugs, pottery and painted tiles were purchased and sent home. Artists were also commissioned to create murals and invited back to Chicago for the installation and to complete the interior decoration.

Because of the wide acceptance of Plaza Proenza, plans are on schedule to redo the rest of Lindo Mexico.

Recessed niches alongside the booths hold native Mexican pottery. Plaid cotton fabric continues the rustic atmosphere.

The booths have colorful ethnic art painted on the sides.

The booth section of the main dining room is slightly raised above the main dining floor. Beautiful blue and cream tiles create a checkerboard design in this area.

Baskets and dried flowers hang from the ceiling, adding rustic charm to the dining room.

Portland Deli

Project Location
Portland, Oregon

Interior Design
ASSOCIATED DESIGN CONSULTANTS, INC.
Sam F. Taylor IV/*Project Manager*
Debbie Munson/*Designer*

Good-bye quarry floor tile, brown wall tile and brown fiberglass tables with orange and yellow accents. Good-bye Hamburgers, Etc. That's what Sam F. Taylor IV, and Debbie Munson said when overhauling the design and image of a 4000-square-foot fastfood restaurant near the entrance of a busy mall. The result? Today, The Portland Deli has a revised menu, a revamped look and a standing-room-only business. The deli serves light meals, mostly sandwiches and salads, to a predominantly female clientele. Carpet replaced the tile, except the main traffic areas. Mini-blinds create a "safe" feeling in the evening and block the sun in the afternoon.

Randomly located structural columns are used as delicate design features that set the tone in the restaurant. By utilizing the columns and adding false columns to bracket large glass panels, areas of the deli are separated, yet remain open. The glass panels feature an etched iris motif, which sets the tone throughout The Portland Deli.

The existing ceiling had incandescent downlights and soffits that didn't go with the new interior. However, because budget was limited, the lights

The deli entrance features fabric draped from one drum-like fixture to another. The end result diffuses light and noise and creates a soft visual.

A view from the solarium of the service counter.

Bleached driftwood and custom tables are welcome comforts to its predominantly female clientele.

An etched iris design on glass panels set the project's theme.

had to stay. Inexpensive ceiling fabric, which softens the harsh ceiling changes and hides sprinkler heads and air diffusers, creates a dramatic effect above. The hanging fabric is placed around large drum-like fixtures. The custom fixtures are large enough in diameter to allow for ventilation and bulb changing. The indirect light is reflected from the ceiling for more intimate lighting. Additionally, the fabric has an added benefit. It acts as a noise buffer.

The soffit above the service counter is dropped to create a friendly atmosphere for patrons. Glass menu boards are actually the backs of vertical storage cabinets used for condiments, tea, napkins, and the like.

The colors in The Portland Deli are soft. Custom tables, bleached driftwood chairs, plants and pastels reflect sophistication and a fresh new image.

Queen Italian Restaurant

Project Location
Brooklyn, New York

Client
Anthony, Pasquino and Vincent Vitiello

Interior Design
T.M. DESIGN & PLANNING
Mandi QuKay/*Designer*
Tom Fisher/*Project Director*
Peter Bystron/*Project Manager*

Contractor
Billy Parlamas Contracting

Photography
John McManas

Queen Italian restaurant has been a tradition in downtown Brooklyn ever since founder, Anthony Vitiello, first opened the doors in September, 1958. For 32 years, the traditional, dark paneled, "red" Italian restaurant served customers some of the finest lunches and dinners found anywhere.

Then in 1990 progress overtook the neighborhood, and the building in which the restaurant was located was scheduled for demolition. The current owners, Anthony's two sons, decided to move the eating establishment to within one block of its original address but to continue their father's legacy with a fresh look. Mandi QuKay of T.M. Design & Planning was approached to give the Queen a "facelift." The two brothers wanted a bright, open, up-to-date envi-

A recessed light cove and a change in materials help to visually separate the cafe and the main dining room.

ronment that would appeal to present as well as future patrons.

The new design of the restaurant incorporates two concepts. The front portion of the 2254 square foot space is the "cafe," where shoppers or theatergoers can stop afterward for pastry and a cappuccino. The larger, rear portion of the space is devoted to dining.

The designer's skillful use of architectural details succeeds in creating the Italian theme. Two teal blue, Doric columns situated beneath a dropped ceiling herald the entrance to the dining area itself. In the middle of the room, a floating structural column was concealed in the same Tuscan base and Doric capital and then topped with a planter to further eclipse its obstrusiveness. The mirrored wall in which the planter ends reflects the column and visually completes the symmetry. A classically Italian arch motif is reiterated in the wall niches, the windows, and the half round backs of the bar stools. The softly arched awnings and the miniature balconies, with their display of Italian foods, evoke the imagery of dining on a plaza in Old World Italy. The awnings also draw attention away from the activity around the doors.

The cafe portion of the 96-seat restaurant features beautiful peach marble table tops and flooring accented by soothing seafoam green chair seats. The marble floor gives way to the custom dining room carpet, which ties the color scheme of emerald green, peach, and seafoam green together in a marbled effect. Wood trim and brass accents recur throughout the space to soften the harsh stucco and marble surfaces.

A modern lighting system composed of recessed downlights, wall washers, and sconces now illuminates the space. Dimmer switches allow the general light level to be adjusted upward or downward according to the time of day and the mood desired.

Everyone in Brooklyn agrees that the Queen will continue to reign as a fine Italian restaurant for many more years to come. Long live the Queen!

The well placed mirrored wall reflects the column structure and opposing side of the room creating symmetry in the space.

Detail of wall niches and miniature balconies complete with their display of Italian foods.

Ralphie's Diner

Project Location
Timonium, Maryland

Interior Design
DORF ASSOCIATES INTERIOR DESIGN INC.
Martin E. Dorf/*Principal, Architect*
Robert McGrath, Lorraine Knapp, Andrea McBride

Photography
Robert Creamer

In recent years, America's love affair with the nostalgic past has boosted the popularity of restaurants that have as their theme the old-fashioned diner. These spaces seem to evoke in all of us memories of what was good and fun about the past and to push into our subconscious the things we do not want to remember. Youngsters who, until now, could not visualize the past are fascinated by the feeling of being transported "back to the future."

Ralphie's Diner, a full-service, three-meal-a-day restaurant located in Timonium, Maryland, certainly proves this "theory of popularity." Restaurateurs Hersh and Michael Pacino, along with Dorf Associates Interior Design Inc., chose the theme of a 1930s-style diner because of its "timeless appeal to all ages 8 to 80." With its location in a new office building complex surrounded by residential neighborhoods, the diner purposely offers something for everyone, including families, white collar workers, teens, and senior citizens.

The design concept for the 6,500 square foot restaurant artfully combined four different operations: the dessert, baked goods, and retail gift counter; the soda fountain, the bar, and the restaurant. The materials and finishes used to create the Art Deco decor are repeated in each area but are combined in varying ways to give each a separate identity. Black and white mosaic tile flooring, mahogany wood, satin aluminum molding, and custom-designed wall sconces are unifying elements that occur throughout.

The dining areas are defined by cove-lit, vaulted ceilings from which hang half-spherical-shaped pendant lights. At the entrance, the bakery and dessert counter affords the office crowd a chance to get a quick roll for breakfast on the way to the office. A white on black mosaic tile floor reverses to black on white to place special emphasis on the retail counter.

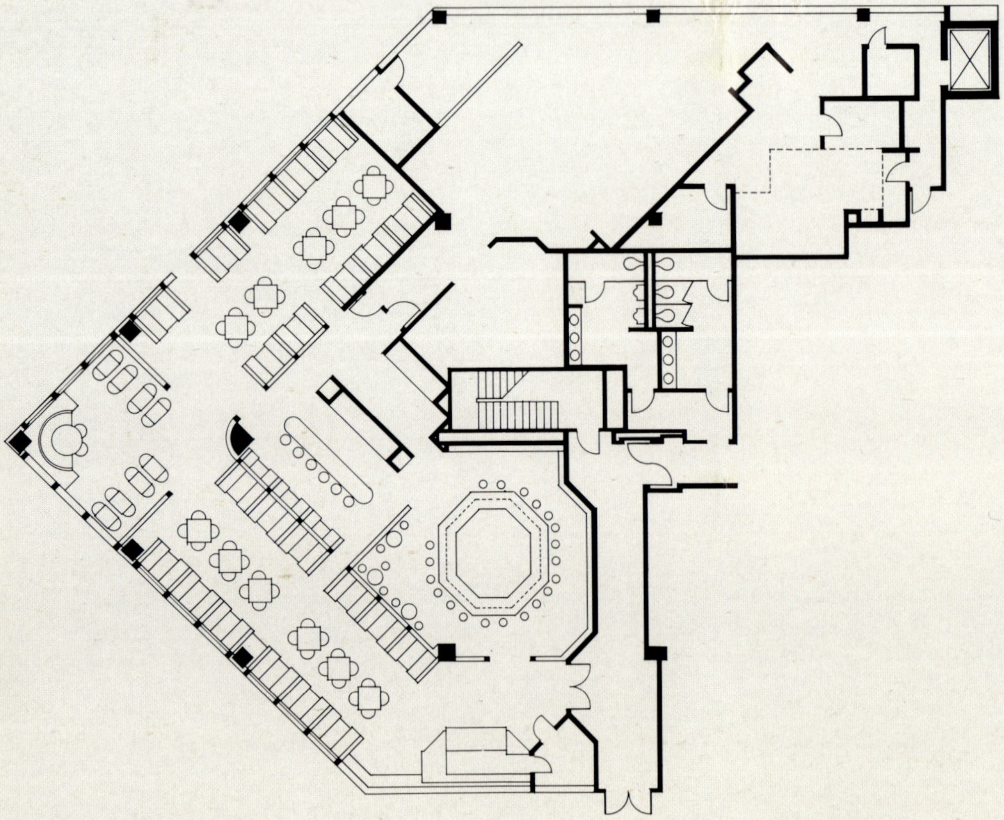

At the entrance to Ralphie's Diner, another Art Deco clock logo made of stainless steel and neon shines over the dessert case.

Souper Salad

Project Location
Boston, Massachusetts

Interior Design
MORRIS NATHANSON DESIGN
Morris Nathanson/*President*
David Jackson/*Designer*
Blase Gallo/*Vice President-Director of Design*
Peter Niemitz/*Vice President*

Photography
WARREN JAGGER PHOTOGRAPHY INC.

Morris Nathanson Design's "express concept" can be summed up in one word, according to its designers: streamline. By incorporating the old with the new, Morris Nathanson, David Jackson, Blase Gallo and Peter Niemitz created a "moving" interior design without the assembly line feeling of a typical fast-food joint.

The top brass at Souper Salad wanted to take the company's approach of serving only fresh health foods, usually served by waitresses, down a slightly different path. The goal was to offer hungry patrons these delicious dishes via self-service and take-out. The designers' approach was toward funky and playful when bringing "humanity to fast food" as their client requested. The colors are somewhat tropical, and the look is centered around a past meets present sleek white.

Hanging white glass pendants, colorful signage, glass front displays and bright neon combine nostalgia and contemporary for a festive, airy result.

A high-ceiling allowed room for a mezzanine level of seating upstairs.

Caffé Spuntino

Project Location
Mineola, New York

Interior Design
DALLAGO INTERIORS
Karen Dallago
Sharon Dallago-Genden

When three experienced restauranteurs and an enthusiastic chef from San Francisco teamed up to create an Italian cafe in Mineola, New York, they wanted something different than the slew of other such eateries nearby. From its cheerful, sophisticated interior by Dallago Interiors Inc. to its varied menu, Caffé Spuntino accomplishes just that.

The challenge for the designers was to create an atmosphere wherein people could feel just as comfortable wearing tennis shorts while eating a pizzotte or wearing a dinner jacket and savoring grilled prawns flown in from the Caribbean. Spuntino in Italian means to pick, another way of saying "a little bit of this and a little of that." The restaurant has become a stopping ground for a cappuccino and dessert, a few appetizers and a drink, or a complete dinner selected from the daily "specials" board.

Caffé Spuntino features an open kitchen—at the request of its owners. The kitchen is separated from the dining

area by a 30-foot counter. Clients waiting to be seated are invited to watch the chefs in action. Although diners can actually watch as they wait for their fresh pasta, the restaurant doesn't lack class or ambiance.

Upon entering the double-level restaurant, clients are greeted with a 10-foot showcase displaying the fresh fish and antipasto selections of the day. At the other end of the dining room, a pastry case tempts diners with fresh desserts made on the premises. A large bar/main station serves as the visual nucleus between the upper and lower levels.

Three "tiers" lead to a skylight, giving the illusion of a higher ceiling.

The lower level, which incorporates the main dining room, is tiled in a custom pattern by the designers. The gridded floor pattern is placed on a 90-degree angle from the tiled kitchen wall. However, an illusion of a 45-degree angle was created by strategic placement of dominating colors, visually pulling entering diners into the restaurant. The same pattern and colors are used on the upper and lower levels of the restaurant. The designers chose colors that would "excite" diners and also be unique. Bright coral moldings house lighting tubes. This adds the illusion of a higher ceiling, while allowing for soft lighting. The triple tier of light opens up to a large skylight. The coral, mauve, gray, aqua and white color accents add to the decor.

The tables' tops are granite-like laminate. The striking design of the chairs complement the other bold design elements. An upper platform off the main dining area was designed to be adaptable. It can be used for an overflow of clients waiting to be seated, an after-hours cappucino and pastry crowd, or for extra dining space.

A colorful contemporary variation of a checkerboard pattern is used on the floor and walls of Caffé Spuntino.

Stanford's American Bar & Grill

Project Location
Providence, Rhode Island

Interior Design
DILEONARDO INTERNATIONAL, INC.
Robert J. DiLeonardo, Ph.D./*President*

Photography
Warren Jagger
PHOTOGRAPHY INC.

Stanford's American Bar and Grill in the Omni Biltmore offers several distinctive dining spaces, each designed by Robert J. DiLeonardo, Ph.D., President, of DiLeonardo International.

The main salon is reminiscent of the 1930s. A French Impressionist mural, brass and black torchiers, upholstered divans, fan back and channel dining chairs make this area the most formal space in Stanford's. The west end of the Salon offers a view of an open kitchen, set behind maple and brass shelves and finely crafted oak cabinets.

The Promenade, at the end of Salon, offers larger tables that can be arranged for large groups at banquet-like settings. An original barrel vaulted ceiling is lined in gold leaf paper and mirrors at either ends. The ceiling links the hotel lobby and street in a pedestrian passageway. A custom tile border provides a decorative accent. Here's the place for a leisurely breakfast, quick lunch or post-theater snack. Its design is relaxed and welcoming.

Just past the Promenade is the lounge where guests can enjoy a European bistro experience. The large bar is the place to get American coffee or expresso in the morning or cocktails in the evening. The food, wine and beer collections are part of the decor. Its interior attracts both a business and social clientele.

In private dining rooms off the Promenade, guests are offered total privacy. Turn-of-the-century side chairs are covered in tan with a "Fortuny" fabric on the backs of chairs in red and gold. These rooms were designed for patrons who want an intimate, elegant setting away from other people and the busy pace of the other dining areas.

T.K. Tripps

Project Location
Winston-Salem, North Carolina

Interior Design
ONE DESIGN CENTER, INC.
Linda Higgins, IBD, ASID/*President and Senior Designer*
Alcira Saca/*Designers*

Photography
RICK ALEXANDER & ASSOCIATES

When T.K. Tripps' management decided to change the 10-restaurant chain's marketing strategy to create a more sophisticated environment, the services of One Design Center, Inc., were called for. The restaurant had been centered, from design to promotional strategies, on its bar business, fun meeting place atmosphere and medium-priced food. It was time to focus on food, while holding onto the existing clientele and festive atmosphere, and establish a new market niche.

Space planning changes included moving the bar to the center of the 6800 square foot layout and decreasing the amount of bar-only seating. This central location eliminates the need for a service bar and is accessible from the main entrance.

Diners in each of the two dining areas to the left and right of the bar have an open view across the restaurant, but remain separate. By alternating levels, ceiling treatments, finishes and furniture, a unique decor is brought to each section. Brick work and brass bring class elements into the airy restaurant. Archways, plants and brightly colored upholstery are interesting design features. Chairs and booths duplicate arch curves.

A view from the entry into separate dining areas.

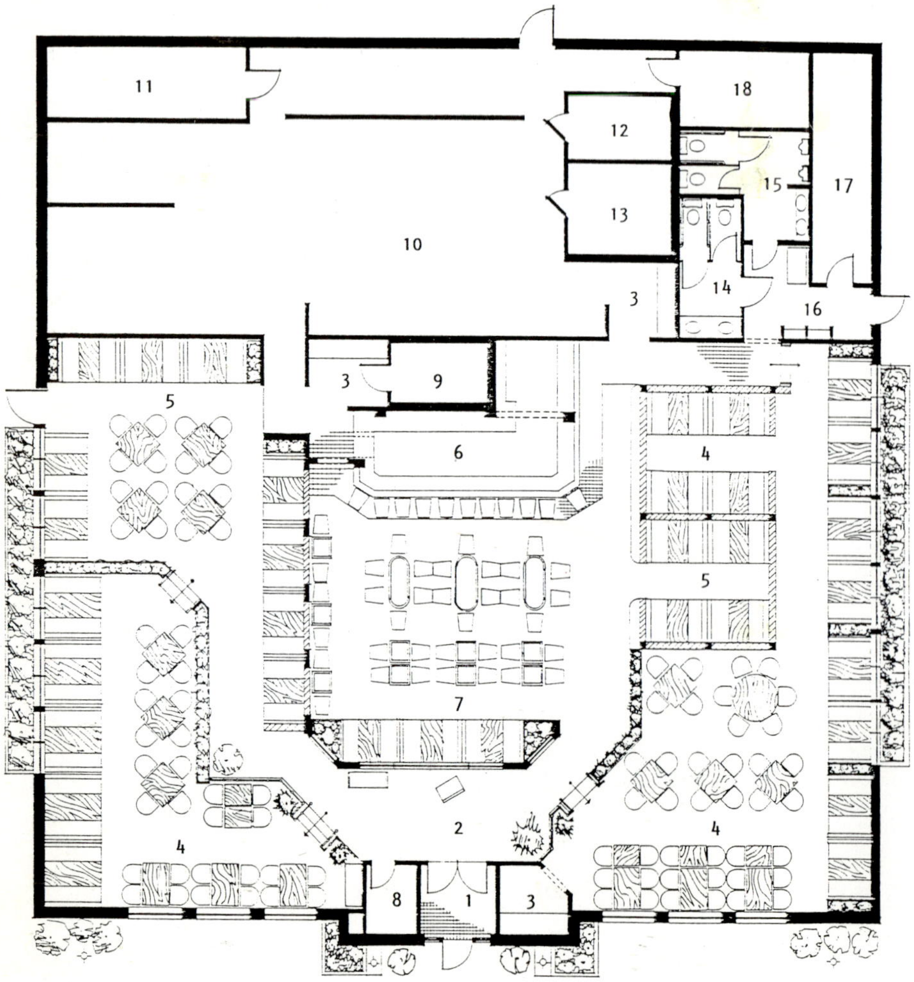
11
18
12
15
17
13
10
3
14
16
3
9
5
6
4
5
7
2
4
4
8
1
3

Private dining booths are made more intimate by full planters and individual hanging lights over tables.

Trapani Pasta Company

Project Location
Clackamas, Oregon

Interior Design
ASSOCIATED DESIGN CONSULTANTS, INC.
Sam F. Taylor IV/*Project Manager*
Dudley Mattocks/*Design Director*

Photography
Roger L. Wagner

When the one and only restaurant in Portland's Clackamus Town Center closed, the mall's developers decided to renovate and put two restaurants in its place. One is the 16′ × 64′ Trapani Pasta Company. Designers Sam F. Taylor IV, and Dudley Mattocks made the best of the space that many would have found too confining. Common seating in the mall made limited seating inside Trapani possible. A bulky, space-wasting dishwasher wasn't installed in the eatery where paper plates and plastic utensils dominate Because the restaurant specializes in fresh, made-on-the-spot dishes, storage space could be downsized.

Much of Trapani's interior is based on illusion. Mirror used on the two dining walls allows the space to open visually, practically doubling its width. Faux marble columns along the long wall of the dining area reduce the length of the restaurant while offering some separation between tables. Tiers of the columns hold silk flowers.

The theme of the restaurant is dramatic—perhaps it's the back lit awnings, neon accents and checkerboard floor that bring a combined taste of a classic malt shop and Italian sidewalk cafe. The curves of a 30-foot serving/cooking counter are covered by white laminate. Black plastic auto trim stripes run the length of the counter and parallel to its black countertop. Backlighting along the service area draws attention to it, rather than the restaurant's narrow layout.

Large photo murals of Trapani dishes flank the menu boards displayed at eye level. Ingredients are listed for the 18- to 35-year-old health conscious clientele. Customers also can view the food on the service line.

Pizza and calzones are prepared at the end of the counter closest to the mall. A menu is also on view to passers-by who may slow to get a better look—or better smell. Trapani includes a small out-of-view working kitchen in the back. It's here that most of the dishes are prepared. A walk-in cooler holds cheese, meat, dough and other items.

A floating celing effect is yet another highlight. White plastic panels framed in red seem to "jump out" of the black painted ceiling from which they're hung. About 20 people can be seated in the restaurant. Black topped tables, complemented by chrome and black stools, are arranged for two or three diners at a time. A condiment and utensil display is set at the back of Trapani. It integrates a trash receptacle. A planter at the front of the eatery doubles as a trash bin.

A backlit awning and stone front catches the attention of shoppers at an Oregon mall.

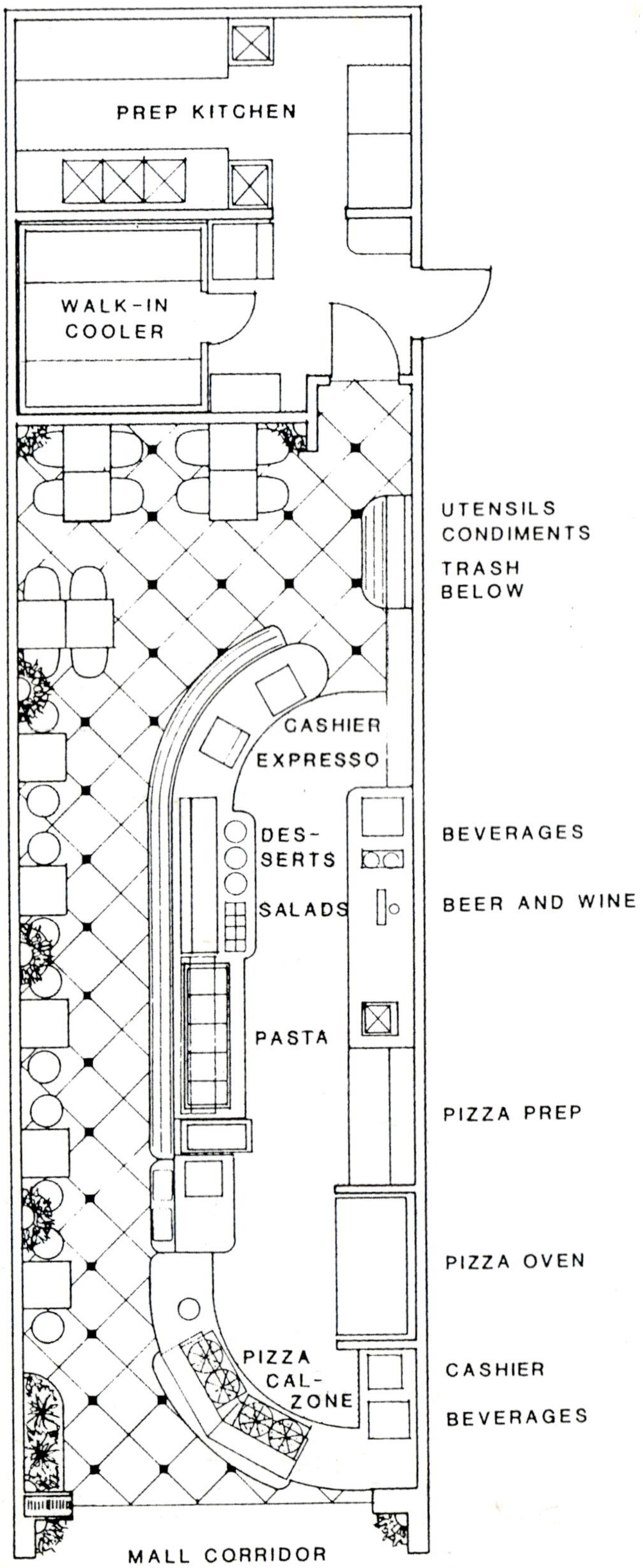
PREP KITCHEN
WALK-IN COOLER
UTENSILS CONDIMENTS
TRASH BELOW
CASHIER
EXPRESSO
DES-SERTS
SALADS
PASTA
BEVERAGES
BEER AND WINE
PIZZA PREP
PIZZA OVEN
PIZZA CAL-ZONE
CASHIER
BEVERAGES
MALL CORRIDOR

Trapani
PASTA COMPA

Trocadero

Project Location
Irvine, California

Interior Design
HATCH DESIGN GROUP
Jeff Hatch, Melinda Shriver

Photography
Don Romero

By using plenty of koa wood, white walls, blue accents and natural light, the design team of Jeff Hatch and Melinda Shriver created a Caribbean plantation house atmosphere in the 3400-square-foot Trocadero restaurant of Irvine, California. It's located in the Irvine Market Place near the local branch of the University of California. The restaurant specializes in gourmet appetizers and tropical drinks.

A 10′ × 10′ skylight, located centrally above the raised eating area, provides natural light throughout the casual interior. Corrugated galvinized metal panels with koa wood beams are used on the ceiling. Painted onto the plaster walls are faux windows looking onto sandy beaches.

The space, which seats 100, is furnished with wicker furniture covered by bright fabrics. Ceiling fans, tropical plants and custom fixtures keep the atmosphere airy—the fixtures are made of koa wood.

Table tops were custom made in Sante Fe, New Mexico: a handpainted goatskin finish under an acrylic finish. Imported fossilized sandstone covers a concrete slab floor in the bar and entry areas. Hardwood oak planks are used in the raised dining area, which includes a piano.

Completing the theme is an open display kitchen with a handmade masonry wood-fired oven which is used in preparing Caribbean dishes.

The raised dining area looking toward the entrance.

The floor of the predominantly all koa wood bar area is fossilized sandstone.

Village Tavern

Project Location
Charlotte, North Carolina

Interior Design
ONE DESIGN CENTER, INC.
Cynthia F. Folds, IBD/*Principal and Senior Designer*
Roger D. Ward, IBD/*Senior Designer*

Photography
Whitney Cox

The Village Tavern in Charlotte, North Carolina, is the third in a chain of full-service restaurants for young professionals in Southeastern cities. The restaurant is located on the first floor of an office building in a corporate park. This meant adapting a successful free-standing plan for Cynthia F. Folds, IBD, and Roger K. Ward, both of whom helped develop the free-standing prototype.

Light woods and simple furniture are used to reflect the simplicity of Southern living. A relaxed upscale atmosphere is the end result. To retain the identity developed in the first two Village Tavern restaurants, the designers chose identical furnishings and architectural detailing. However, darker wood finishes and a bold black and white tile parquet flooring add a more sophisticated feel to the contemporary, uptown setting.

An open decor throughout creates an openness that lets patrons see into other areas. The bar is set along the

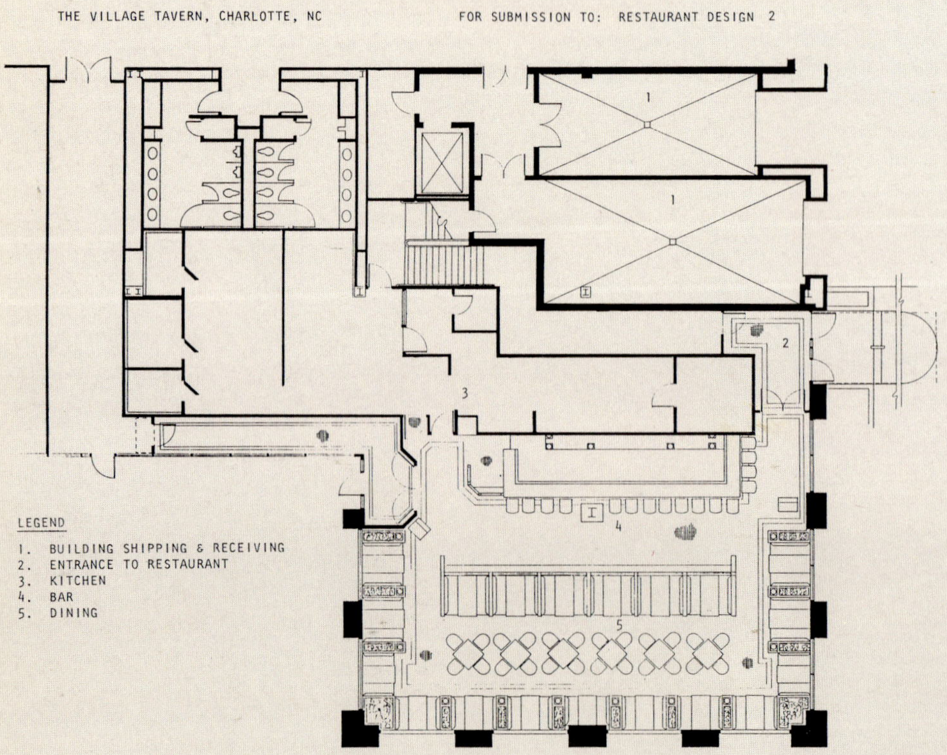

A black and white checkerboard floor nicely contrasts the dark wood and light fabrics used in a more contemporary Village Tavern.

Detailed columns separate booths, adding a feeling of privacy.

back wall, separated from the dining area. The main entrance provides access to the bar and dining spots, as does the kitchen.

An interesting wood ceiling treatment figures prominently in the interior decor. Wood columns also lend interesting visual appeal, while serving as dividers between booths.

The Village Tavern's central gathering place.

Village Tavern

Project Location
Greensboro, North Carolina

Interior Design
ONE DESIGN CENTER, INC.
Cynthia F. Folds, IBD/*Principal and Senior Designer*
Roger D. Ward, IBD/*Senior Designer*

Photography
Whitney Cox

If you took a British tavern and tossed in a lot of southern flavor, complete with a "back-porch" atmosphere and upscale, casual decor, you'd have Village Tavern. Designers Cynthia F. Folds, IBD, and Roger D. Ward, IBD, selected architectural details and finishes that emphasize a soft, open feeling. Teal wallcoverings and upholstery, light woods and simple furnishings contrast the dark wood floor. Surface materials, chosen carefully for ease of maintenance, contribute to the comfortable interior.

The owner of the full-service restaurant, one of a few existing Village Taverns in the Southeast, requested an interior that would allow his young professional patrons to see and be seen, yet still feel a sense of privacy when dining. In fact, owner Scott Richardson further challenged the designers to develop a prototype for future free-standing Village Tavern locations.

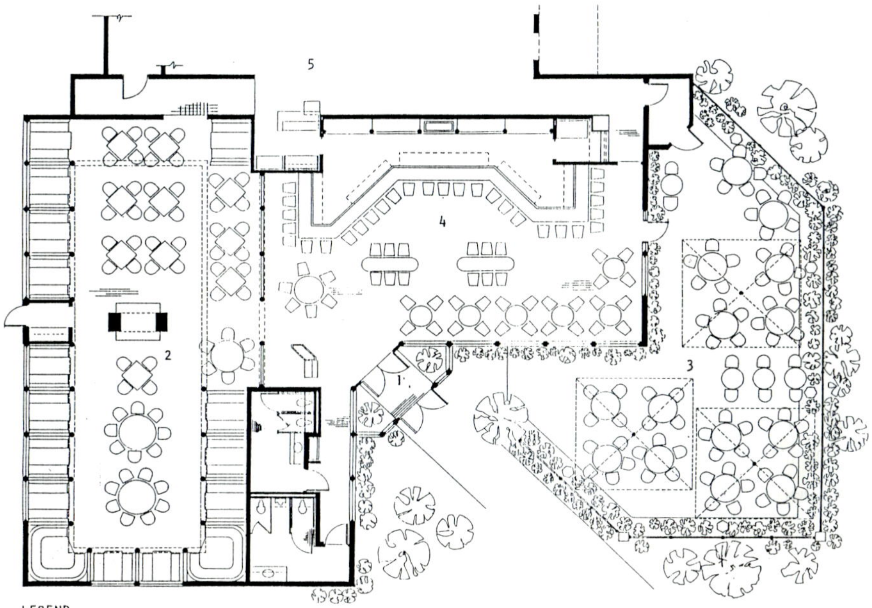

LEGEND
1. MAIN ENTRANCE
2. DINING AREA
3. PATIO
4. BAR
5. KITCHEN

An L-shaped floor plan puts the bar at the back, adjacent to dining areas. The booths and tables are arranged to provide a choice of seating, while "directing" traffic flow. On the other side of the bar is an outdoor patio.

The restaurant's main entrance is situated for direct access to the bar and dining areas. Placing the kitchen across the back of the building provides direct access from the kitchen to the dining areas, bar and patio.

Ceiling treatments and columns dominate and visually separate areas of the 6625 square foot Village Tavern. Along the parts of the ceiling shutter-like woodworking adds elements of a Southern home. Columns set between booths create a more intimate dining experience.

Light wood furniture contrasts the dark floor in the restaurant's dining area.

An outdoor patio—a variation of a Southern porch.

Columns separate booths for more personal, private dining.

Ceiling fans, bleached wood tables and chairs, and teal upholstery create an airy ambiance in a Southern variation of a British pub.

Williams Restaurant

Project Location
Williams Restaurant

Project Location
Bothell, Washington

Interior Design
ASSOCIATED DESIGN CONSULTANTS, INC.
Sam F. Taylor/*Project Manager*
Lee Holcomb/*Design Coordinator*

Photography
Dick Busher

When employees working at a business park in Bothell, Washington, break for lunch, many of them make a break for Williams Restaurant and Lounge. The idea behind the coffee shop's art deco interior was to make it so inviting that workers would be encouraged to return for weekday dinners, perhaps even bringing along their families, and on weekends. The design also had to be able to accommodate groups of six to ten people and be in good taste for its white-collar clientele.

A tile mosaic border begins in the entry and draws patrons through glass etched doors into a waiting area. Upon entering, they are greeted by a custom "juke box" that is actually a pastry case. It's refrigerated with a Styrofoam and wood frame that is covered with a stretch fabric. To avoid traffic problems, the case is accessible only from the back. The tile mosaic found in the entry is repeated as outlining for the circular booths located on either side of the dessert bar. It's even repeated in the floor-to-ceiling tiled restrooms.

A juke box of desserts welcomes arriving patrons.

Black palm trees etched into the area behind the bar lend a tropical touch.

Wonderland Greyhound Park

Project Location
Revere, Massachusetts

Interior Design
MORRIS NATHANSON DESIGN, INC.
Morris Nathanson/*President*
Peter Niemitz/*Vice President*
Blase Gallo/*Vice President–Director of Design*

Photography
WARREN JAGGER PHOTOGRAPHY INC.

When Morris Nathanson Design, Inc. began refurbishing the entire Wonderland dog track, the owner stipulated that the park remain open everyday throughout all the design and construction phases. The owner of the track didn't just want a few new colors and reorganized betting and dining areas. The plan was for a major overhaul that would keep the present clientele faithful and attract a whole new crowd.

The design team opted for a new grandstand, food courts, seating areas, individual restaurants and bars, and new betting areas. The three restaurants alone encompass 14000 square feet.

Durability, easy maintenance and safety were the chief design concerns. A stippled rubber floor tile was specified only after days of testing. Standard size ceramic tiles were chosen for walls in bright white, black and red to create an upbeat and up-to-date look.

The idea behind the renovation and its restaurants was to create a pleasant environment for all levels of comfort. Special attention was made to attract a strong middle class crowd—from high rollers to business professionals.

The track includes a "clubhouse restaurant" where patrons order food at a service counter and then return to cafeteria-style seats. Neon is used to create a fun, contemporary atmosphere. Tile here is used extensively—on columns, the floors, counter facades and walls. Patterns vary from the classic checkerboard to a more flamboyant mixture of large and small tiles.

The track also includes a deli, completed in darker, more serious tones. Television screens are featured prominently so clients won't miss any of the racing action. The lighting is dimmed for more atmosphere.

A third bar/restaurant combination features a simple decor, in more subtle, yet bright, colors. Laminate counters and accents, and a wall of big-screen television sets lend a relaxed atmosphere.

The entire remodeling of the track took the design team one year. Not a single day at the races was lost.

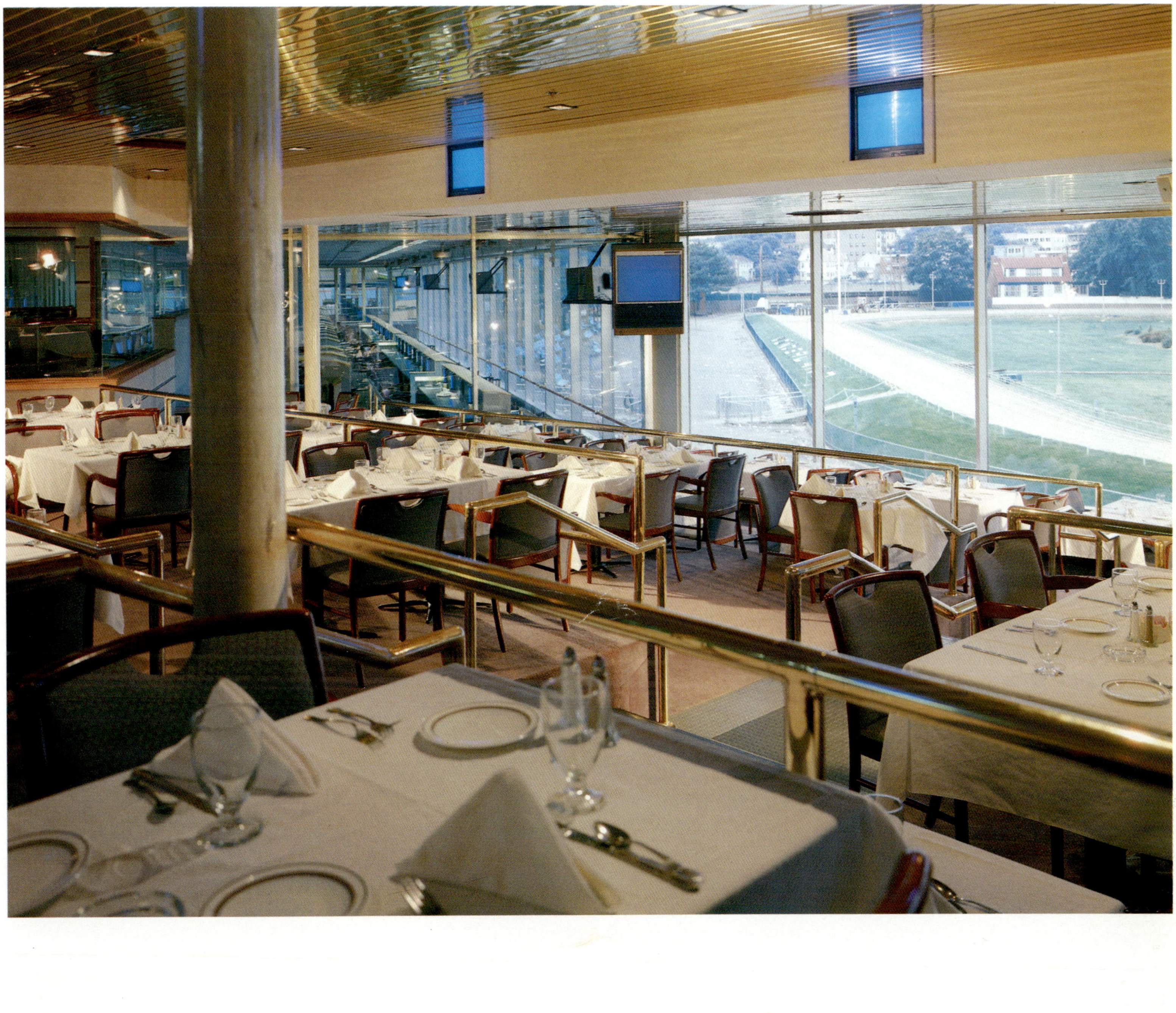

Zuni Grill

Project Location
Irvine, California

Interior Design
HATCH DESIGN GROUP
Jeff Hatch, Rick McCormack, Jackie Hanson

Photography
Don Romero

With respect to the American Indian tribe of its namesake, Zuni Grill, a cozy 154 seat upscale eatery, transcends its patrons deep into the heart of the desert Southwest. Formidable faux-granite blocks topped with onyx-like panels serve as an entry to the space, simulating a cave dwelling. Further enhancing the primal design, raw-colored concrete sweeps through the space at the floor level, only to be stopped by large broken fragments of flagstone. Hand-weathered and painted wall surfaces of sunset hues cast a warm glow, broken at a midway point to the ceiling, exposing rough edges. Protruding beams of burnished metal layered across the space serve as the rough ceiling, leaving the duct work beyond well-hidden. Jagged glass pieces throughout add yet another time honored material to the scene. To soften the elements, heavy woven fabrics, reminiscent of thick Indian blankets, were used

Earthtone colors and natural materials create a southwestern atmosphere.

on seating, accompanied by iridescent vinyls and stone flecked carpet in other areas. Dining tables, with whimsical pictographs, and brightly colored abstract art pieces add to the spirit of the environment. To further invoke a cave-like setting, the space is dimly lit with fanciful lighting of metal, mesh and glass. It is the unison of these natural materials with contemporary treatments that allows the restaurant its socially "Sante-Fean attitude," while at the same time granting every patron a glimpse at the spirit of the Zuni people.

Hand-weathered stone creates a "cave dwelling" feeling. In addition, colorful artwork graces the walls, and even the floor to promote the "Zuni" theme.

Iridescent vinyl upholstery and stone-flecked carpeting enhance the natural materials used in this vibrant interior.

Even the dishware utilizes desert colors.

Abstract Indian art is well-lighted, thus creating an impactful design statement.

The undulating stone wall separates the bar area from the entrance.